Sofia Van Matre Bompiani

Italian Explorers in Africa

Sofia Van Matre Bompiani

Italian Explorers in Africa

ISBN/EAN: 9783744751575

Printed in Europe, USA, Canada, Australia, Japan

Cover: Foto ©ninafisch / pixelio.de

More available books at **www.hansebooks.com**

GAETANO CASATI

The Leisure Hour Library.—New Series

III.

ITALIAN EXPLORERS
IN AFRICA

BY

SOFIA BOMPIANI

WITH MANY PORTRAITS

THE RELIGIOUS TRACT SOCIETY
56 PATERNOSTER ROW, 65 ST. PAUL'S CHURCHYARD
AND 164 PICCADILLY

1891

Oxford
HORACE HART, PRINTER TO THE UNIVERSITY

PREFACE.

THE substance of these sketches appeared in the *Leisure Hour* in the years 1888 and 1890. At that time they were the first connected account of Italian Exploration in Africa which had appeared in this country. The suggestion was made in the Journal of the Royal Geographical Society that they would serve a useful purpose if reprinted. With this object in view the author has carefully revised and in several cases considerably enlarged the original sketches. Resident in Rome, she has had special opportunities of access to the records of the Italian Geographical Society, and for consulting other reliable sources of information. It is hoped that the list of portraits, which is as complete as it could be made, will give additional value to the volume.

CONTENTS.

CHAP.		PAGE
I.	INTRODUCTION	11
II.	GIOVANNI MIANI	14
III.	CARLO PIAGGIA	21
IV.	ROMOLO GESSI AND LAKE ALBERT	27
V.	DOCTOR PELLEGRINO MATTEUCCI	43
VI.	ORAZIO ANTINORI AND HIS COMPANIONS	54
VII.	CECCHI AND CHIARINI AMONG THE EQUATORIAL LAKES	71
VIII.	DR. TRAVERSI	91
IX.	RECENT ITALIAN EXPEDITIONS IN NORTH-EASTERN AFRICA	101
X.	CARDINAL MASSAJA	117
XI.	PASTOR G. P. WEITZECKER AND ITALIAN MISSIONARY ENTERPRISE	126
XII.	COUNT PIETRO DI BRAZZA	139
XIII.	GIACOMO DI BRAZZA, ATTILIO PECILE, AND PIETRO ANTONELLI	154
XIV.	GIUSEPPE HAIMANN AND GIACOMO BOVE	162
XV.	LUIGI ROBECCHI BRICCHETTI'S JOURNEY ACROSS LIBYA	169
XVI.	GAETANO CASATI	183

LIST OF ILLUSTRATIONS.

	PAGE
GAETANO CASATI	*Frontispiece*
GIOVANNI MIANI IN ARAB COSTUME	14
CARLO PIAGGIA	21
ROMOLO GESSI	27
PELLEGRINO MATTEUCCI	43
ORAZIO ANTINORI	54
MENILEK	56
THE QUEEN OF SHOA	71
ANTONIO CECCHI	77
CHIARINI	82
GUSTAVUS BIANCHI	101
CAPTAIN GIULIETTI	102
CARLO COCASTELLI DI MONTIGLIO	104
COUNT SALIMBENI	109
MAJOR PIANO	113
COUNT TANCREDI SAVOIROUX	115
CARDINAL MASSAJA	117
G. P. WEITZECKER	126
COUNT PIETRO DI BRAZZA	139
GIACOMO DI BRAZZA	154
COUNT PIETRO ANTONELLI	158
LUIGI ROBECCHI BRICCHETTI	169

ITALIAN EXPLORERS IN AFRICA.

CHAPTER I.

INTRODUCTION.

THE history of Italian explorations in Africa during the past twenty years is an index of the vigorous life which animates the nation now united under a just and progressive government.

It was not enough to blend in one the seven states into which *il bel paese* had been divided; to wrest from the Pope his temporal power; to restore the finances; establish schools; create an army, and teach a common language to the dialect-speaking inhabitants, from Venice to Sicily; but Italians have tracked the waves of the Eastern and Western oceans, explored the icy regions of the North, tried to solve the enigmas of the Antarctic Continent, and laid down their noble lives in the malarious forests and burning deserts of Africa.

Exalted rivalry with England and America—the models of young Italy—impelled them to undertake these explorations. They knew that Africa beguiled them to exile and death; but the yet undiscovered lakes, the frowning mountains, the unknown rivers, attracted them and inspired them with ambition to plant the Italian banner and leave their own names inscribed on some part of the Dark Continent.

After the great explorations of Livingstone, Stanley, Cameron, and Nachtigal, a new phase of African exploration began; and fresh impulse was given to it by the foundation of the International African Society by the King of Belgium, which proposed to explore Equatorial, Central, and Eastern Africa, Abyssinia, and the country of the Somali.

This region between the White Nile and Cape Guardafui, including the basin of the Blue Nile, the peninsula of the Somali and Shoa, which is a part of Abyssinia, has chiefly engaged the attention of Italian explorers since 1875.

Antinori, Cecchi, Chiarini, Piaggia, Gessi, Matteucci, Bianchi, and Martini, not only aimed to found a station in the Shoa and open routes of commerce from there to the coast, but to penetrate south-west to the equatorial lakes over a region even yet unexplored.

But this was not the only sphere of action for the Italian explorers.

Long before the expedition sent out by the Roman Geographical Society, in 1875, Miani had penetrated to the heart of Africa, and left his wearied frame to repose in Mambettù. Romolo Gessi, later, as an officer of the Egyptian Army, under heroic Gordon, ascended the White Nile, and fought a knightly battle for the extinction of slavery. Piaggia lived alone among the savages of Niam-Niam; and Matteucci and Massari crossed the continent in a south-westerly direction from the Red Sea to the mouth of the Niger.

Princes and peasants of Italy gave their sons to solve the mighty secrets of a land so near that it almost touches the southern coast of Sicily, and yet so utterly unknown; white-bearded old men went out to end their days in the enchanting wildernesses; some were enslaved, some were imprisoned and starved on the Nile by the long-armed aquatic plants; some bore the germs of fatal diseases to the borders of home. and died on the very threshold of glory.

GIOVANNI MIANI IN ARAB COSTUME.

CHAPTER II.

GIOVANNI MIANI.

BEFORE Speke discovered Lake Victoria, the source of the Nile, Giovanni Miani the Venetian had penetrated to within a few miles of it, and left his name carved upon a giant tamarind-tree. Under this tree he held counsel with the natives, who, instead of telling him, as they afterwards told Speke and Baker, that the Nile, or Meri, issued from a great lake a few days' march beyond, gave him false information and diverted him from his purpose of pressing onward.

Speke saw the name of Miani carved on the tamarind-tree in his celebrated journey from

Zanzibar to the central lakes, and from them to the Nile.

The life of Miani was one of sadness and disappointment from the cradle to the grave. Born near Venice in 1810, he was first a wood-carver, then artist, then musician; and when the events of 1848 drew him into the vortex of political life, he was exiled from Italy. This was the beginning of his travels in Africa, which continued without intermission until his death in 1872.

After many journeys in Lower Egypt, Miani, in 1859—while noble-hearted Livingstone was exploring in Southern Africa—undertook his first expedition up the Nile. But all of his companions died of fever at Khartoum, and he was obliged to seek others in that city, with whom he continued the journey to Gondokoro and some distance beyond.

He encountered perils from the hostility of the savages, from the malarious climate, from the rocks and terrible aquatic plants on the rivers, and was finally compelled to return because his escort refused to follow him.

Miani made a second and a third journey up the Nile to catch elephants, procuring money for future expeditions by the sale of the ivory. The last of these journeys, from Gondokoro to the country of the Galuffi, is one of the boldest explorations in the Nile region, as he was obliged to open the way for his people by force, through the lands of the natives, and found the streams difficult to cross on account of the rains. He lived in a continual bath; and fought a battle with a tribe of natives, killing the king. The extreme point he reached (sixty miles from Lake Albert, a small lake connected with Victoria) is marked on many maps of the interior of Africa by the tamarind-tree upon which he carved his name. Undaunted by the ill-success of this expedition, Miani, on his return to Cairo, organised another, and left for the Upper Nile, but, from unknown causes, soon returned and went to Europe, where he was welcomed by several monarchs and decorated by Victor Emanuel. At the age of fifty-nine he was nominated by the Khedive Director of the Zoological Garden of Khartoum, and might have ended his days there in peace and luxury. But the desire for exploration urged him to again ascend the mysterious river, the sources of which had, in the meantime, been in part, but not wholly, discovered by Speke, Grant, and Baker.

The journey to Bakangoi, ten days beyond Mambettù, undertaken when he was sixty-one years of age and in very ill-health, considering his age, infirmities, the difficulties of the way through an unexplored region, and his limited means, is one of the boldest on record, and ranks him among the bravest of the African explorers. He left Khartoum in company with some Vekils, or agents of a commercial house, who went in search of ivory.

They ill-treated, and on one occasion even abandoned him in the midst of a cannibal tribe, and when, to their surprise, he succeeded in overtaking them, they exclaimed, ' Any other man would have died if left as you were.' The loss of a part of the copious notes and maps of Miani in a fire, and of the remainder from the carelessness of the Vekils, was fatal to his fame as an African traveller. The few disconnected pages which were brought back to Rome by a faithful native are evidently only a small part of his observations. The region traversed by Miani had not at that time been visited by any European, as his road in going to Mambettù was more to the east than that taken afterwards by the German traveller Schweinfurth.

The lost notes of his journey of four months with the Vekils to the south and west of Mambettù are those most lamented, as in this journey he visited territory afterwards described by Livingstone and Schweinfurth.

Although Miani, deceived by the natives, failed to discover Lake Albert, to which he was so near, he yet on his map placed the source of the Nile only three degrees east of the great Lake Victoria, discovered by Speke, and below it wrote, 'If after my death some honest man shall discover the source of the Nile, to which I was so near, let him at least say that I pointed it out.' Other notes reveal the travail of his soul on these lonesome and difficult journeys. 'Without great sacrifices we cannot honour our country. The journey is long, weary, terrible, and requires courage, strength, constancy, means, and knowledge.'

This was the last journey of the intrepid old man. Worn by the annoyances of the Vekils, and distressed by the cruelties to the slaves which he saw, Miani preferred to be left alone with only his loquacious parrots and mute dogs for company. As he lay, weak and abandoned, under the shade of the giant trees, his eyes were always turned in the direction from which he expected another company of Vekils, with whom he travelled the last few months of his life.

Miani was admired by all the travellers who have ventured into that part of Africa. Speke and Baker mention him with enthusiastic praise, and Schweinfurth, who knew him well, even calls him a second Marco Polo. He died in November, 1872, at the village Numa, near the country of the Niam-Niam, and was buried by his escort in a grave which he himself had caused to be dug.

His last written words are sorrowful: 'I am prostrated by the cough and fever, by the grief of an unsuccessful journey, and the loss of magnificent collections which the Vekils would not give me men to carry. I have no more writing-paper. My servants kiss my hands and say, "May God preserve your life!" Farewell, bright hopes! Farewell, Italy, for whose liberty I fought! Is there a recompense for such suffering?'

The marvellous journey of Stanley, by which he discovered the sources of the Congo and identified it with the Lualaba of Livingstone, proved the truth of Miani's observations made in the same region five years before. The Sultan of Bakangoi informed Miani that at the west of his kingdom was a very large river called Birma-Macongo, which, farther south, became a lake, upon the shores of which lived the tribe Gango, or Congo.

The map made by Miani places this river in the

identical locality indicated by Stanley, who found it there ten miles wide, with every appearance of being a lake.

One of the objects of Miani, Schweinfurth, and Piaggia was the collection or study of rare animals and unknown races of men. They write to each other to seek the flying-dog and the gorilla, and to bring away, if possible, pigmies from Mambettù [1]. The Vekils told Miani one day that they were going to the land of the pigmies in search of ivory. 'These words,' he said, 'made me forget all my troubles.' Probably the account of this journey was destroyed, but the fact of his having given his watch for two boys is recorded, and these Akkàs were sent to Italy with the relics of his papers and collections. They were adopted by a nobleman of Verona, who had them instructed in the Italian language and the elementary studies, as well as in music. They retained the characteristics of the savage—thoughtless mirth, malicious pleasure in mimicking or annoying others, hatred at slight provocation, and lying. One of these Akkàs died recently, but the other bids fair to have a long life, and to endure the cold climate of the north of Italy. They learned easily, but as quickly forgot, remembering almost nothing of their native language and country.

The German traveller Schweinfurth visited them at Palazzo Minescalchi, in Verona, and again expressed his conviction that they were specimens of a race of about the size of the Esquimaux.

[1] The Akkà, called by the cannibal Niam-Niam, the Tikki-tikki are pigmies, said by Schweinfurth to consist of twelve tribes.

Many ancient writers hinted at the existence of pigmy tribes in the torrid region of Africa, near the source of the Nile, but until these Akkàs were found by Miani, and others afterwards by Schweinfurth, these tales were considered fabulous, and men of small stature were believed to exist only in the Arctic regions. It is now certain that pigmy tribes exist in the equatorial region of Africa in the midst of a luxuriant nature and beside peoples of ordinary stature.

CARLO PIAGGIA.

CHAPTER III.

CARLO PIAGGIA.

AFTER Miani, one of the most attractive characters among the Italian explorers in Africa is Carlo Piaggia. His love for the natives, and fearlessness of them, and his romantic visit of twenty-six months among the cannibal Niam-Niam, rank him nearer Livingstone than any other Italian. He was a martyr of science and an apostle of civilisation, who, without special studies, succeeded by the mere force of will and love of exploration in winning admiration. Piaggia was born near Lucca, in 1827, in a humble condition of life, and at the age of twenty-two went to Africa in consequence of a severe domestic affliction which rendered home wearisome to his active spirit. In Egypt he exercised various manual arts, his skill in all of which was afterwards useful in his lonely life among the savages. At home he had been a miller, afterwards in Alexandria he was a bookbinder, a gardener, a hatter, and a carpet-maker; but the chase was his delight, and he made money by killing rare animals and afterwards preparing them for sale. In this way during his twenty-five years of travel he defrayed nearly all his expenses, which, compared with those of other travellers, were small.

Piaggia was an explorer by instinct, urged on to privations and fatigues by an insatiable longing to discover the secrets of Africa. His principal journeys were made alone, with little money, and without other object than study and the hope of doing good to the natives, whom he loved with paternal affection. Wherever he went he left a reputation for goodness and modesty, and was as much beloved by the cannibals of Central Africa as by the learned of Europe. Although he never had the culture of schools, his knowledge was superior to that of many scientific men, and his life during the explorations was a continual study and fatigue. He made his shoes from the skins of the buffalo, the rhinoceros, or the elephant; he made his hats, coats, and shirts; sharpened his arms, made keys, repaired guns, built huts, made traps for lions or hippopotami, and collections of plants, animals, and insects to take back with him to Europe. His thin, sad, yet benevolent face, and slightly bent and weary form, told of those labours, of the tropical heats he had borne, of the agony of expected death from savages or lions, of the sadness of lonely evenings without a light. He never voluntarily looked at his emaciated arms and legs, and often said that he journeyed with less impediment than any other traveller, and that his shadow was thinner on African soil.

In the long sojourn among the Africans he had almost forgotten his native Tuscan, and having from want of company acquired the habit of thinking much and talking little, his speech was not fluent. The adventures of a year would often be condensed into fifty words—simple, modest, but vivid and true.

All his illustrations were drawn from the wild life of the forest. 'I have seen dark days, dear lady, and shed so many tears, that if they were all together it would make much mud.'

This odd idea was only a remembrance of a baby elephant that, when its mother was killed by the hunter, stood still for many hours, groaning and weeping till the earth all round was wet and muddy.

Kindness was the means by which Piaggia, like David Livingstone, won the hearts of the savages, and he could at any time have returned to the places where he had lived. His voice was soft, but the heart within his fragile form was heroic. At one time the savages, thinking him a wizard, had determined to kill him. Seated upon the trunk of a tree, with a tortured heart but unmoved countenance, he reasoned with them in a strange language from early morning till evening, convincing them at last that they would lose more than they would gain by his death. They finally concluded that he was innocent, and went away without saluting; while the poor traveller crept, famished and worn, to his cabin, and threw himself on the ground in a paroxysm of tears.

The most remarkable of his journeys was made in 1863 to the country of the Niam-Niam, where he was escorted by eighty Egyptian soldiers. Having advanced, and asked hospitality of the chief, Piaggia sent away the soldiers, and established himself among these children of the forest, with whom he remained alone twenty-six months. His cabin was for days surrounded by the people, as he was the first white man whom they had seen. Their gestures and shouts of surprise when he took off his shoes and showed his white feet, when he lit a match, or sat down to write, were at the same time pitiful and ludicrous. The women especially showed curiosity, and often seated themselves in a circle around to study him.

'Where did you come from, white man? You do not belong to the earth, because you are not black. You must have come from the air!'

The gift of a piece of coloured muslin to a young girl brought all the women around him to beg for some article of dress, or even a bit of his own costume. The sleeves of his coat, the pantaloons below the knees, the pockets, the brim of his hat, they thought were useless to him, and might serve to dignify them. The time at last came when, the collections of Piaggia being complete, and the longing for home overcoming his resolution, this idyl ended.

The days of dry weather had been filled with pleasant work, and the time then seemed brief; but the sleepless nights, when the full moon lighted the woods around his cabin, and the weary droppings from the thatched roof in the rainy season, made him feel his loneliness. One night he told Tombo, the chief, that he must leave them at dawn.

But Tombo cried, 'The stranger white man is going away!' and all the court was soon awake, the women jumping and waving their arms in sign of grief; and they would not let him go until he had promised soon to return. A great crowd was about him in the morning. The women begged for his long hair, which he had not cut for two years, to divide among them and tie about their waists.

From sickness and famine Piaggia on these journeys often believed his last hour come.

'I cannot tell you how often I have recommended my soul to God,' he says. 'All is ended. I shall die here. Good-bye to all; good-bye to everything.'

But the hardy soul conquered the fainting body, and he lived when a less courageous man would have despaired and died.

Eight journeys were made by Piaggia, chiefly on the Upper Nile and the adjacent countries. The important exploration made in 1876 under the orders of Colonel Gordon, and with Romolo Gessi, was his sixth voyage, and his orders were to explore the river that connects Lake Albert with Lake Victoria, while Gessi circumnavigated the former.

They were provided with two iron sail-boats, thirty feet long, that could be taken in pieces, and with an escort of Egyptian soldiers.

The Italian explorers suffered great fatigue on this journey, and at one time were several days without food. Piaggia obtained it from the wondering savages gathered on the shores by landing with only one servant and advancing unarmed. The natives, at first disposed to be hostile, received him kindly when they saw him caress and throw beads to their children, and provisioned him for several days.

After three months spent in exploring this river, which diverges from Lake Albert near its exit into the White Nile—three months of immense fatigue; of daily efforts to pacify the rebellious soldiers with him; of experience of earthquakes, when the papyrus on the banks of the river waved as if moved by the wind; of journeys through deadly marshes; of encounters with lions and pythons, crocodiles and hippopotami—Piaggia met Gessi, and they returned together to Khartoum.

In 1879 we find him established at Famaca, in Abyssinia, where he built a cabin and lived, much beloved, among the natives, for nine months. From thence as a base he went forward into Galla, hoping to unite with Cecchi and Chiarini, then in prison there, but tidings of the death of Chiarini and the rescue of Cecchi by Bianchi caused him to return.

Piaggia died near Fadasi, at the beginning of another journey to Central Africa, undertaken with a young Hollander named Schumer.

PASHA ROMOLO GESSI.

CHAPTER IV.

ROMOLO GESSI AND LAKE ALBERT.

WHILE Miani and Piaggia travelled modestly alone in Africa, with small means and almost unknown, Romolo Gessi, of Ravenna, traversed the Egyptian possessions and fought battles to suppress slavery, with thousands of soldiers under his command. Gessi was of medium stature and iron frame, with chestnut hair and beard; his eye was bright; his speech prompt and indicative of indomitable will and extraordinary energy; and his soul was animated by the noblest motives. He was one of the heroes of Italy who, although acting as a colonel for the Khedive of Egypt, was never forgotten by his countrymen. At first a merchant, and afterwards engaged in the mercantile marine,

Gessi finally threw himself with ardour into African explorations, his first achievement being the circumnavigation of Lake Albert.

While Carlo Piaggia left him at the mouth of this lake to explore the river, Gessi sailed with a few soldiers and natives around the shores of the lake discovered by Samuel Baker, but never before circumnavigated.

The object which animated Gessi in all of the difficult journeys, the perilous battles, the sufferings and famine he endured, was the abolition of the slave-trade. He entered the service of Ismail Pasha with this end in view, the exploration being a secondary object. He believed the day not far distant when humanity would triumph in Central Africa, and the unhappy tribes there would be relieved from their sufferings. Added to this was the desire, shared with so many explorers of all nations, to fully solve the mystery of the sources of the Nile.

The expedition sent out by the Khedive with the double aim of exploring the Upper Nile and of liberating that region from slavery, was commanded by Colonel Gordon. His staff consisted of seven persons, of whom Gessi was one, but this number was soon reduced to two, by the poisonous air, by famine, and hardships. The river at times in their excursions was so narrow that the boat-wheels touched either shore, and then an immense low plain would spread far away, covered with reeds, papyrus and aquatic plants, and strewn here and there with human bodies in a state of putrefaction. This had evidently been a wide lake in the rainy season, where the waters of the river extended. Gessi and his companions, all suffering from fever, retreated gladly from the place. Like Livingstone and Gordon, he hated the slave-trade, and suppressed it wherever he went. By the orders of Gordon, Gessi took possession of the trade in ivory for the Egyptian Government, this being used as a cloak for their iniquities by the slave-dealers.

In March, 1876, Gessi, accompanied by Piaggia, left Colonel Gordon, to explore Lake Albert.

On his return from the circumnavigation of Lake Albert, one of the most daring and successful explorations ever made in Africa, Gessi, finding that he received the lowest decoration in the gift of the Egyptian Government, while all the other Europeans in the service received the higher ones, resigned his commission and did not re-enter the army until two years later, when Gordon needed his services to subdue Suleiman, on the Bar-Ghasal. He went in the meantime to Italy, where he was received with great honour by the Roman Geographical Society, and decorated for the exploration of Lake Albert with the gold medal. It was especially important for the economical and political interests of Egypt to solve the problem of this mysterious lake, as if the Nile was found to issue from it, the Egyptian Soudan, by means of the great river, might be extended to the Equator.

Gordon sent two distinguished officers of the English army to explore the lake, but one only reached Dufli, and the other Wadelay, returning to Khartoum unsuccessful. The arduous enterprise was then confided to Gessi. Its very beginning was difficult, requiring the services of one thousand natives to transport a steamer and two iron boats, left in pieces by Baker at Gondokoro, overland to Dufli. The way lay over high mountains, across streams and through thick, pathless woods. He started from Dufli with the two boats, meeting contrary winds and passing floating islands formed by the aquatic plants. These islands are often twelve or fifteen feet in depth and miles in length, and are liable to change their places, going before the wind at four or five miles an hour, so that no map of the stream can be exact. They caused Gessi to lose the way several times before finding the mouth of the lake. On the banks of the Nile and of the lake he encountered many tribes of natives. Some of the inhabitants fled at the approach of the boats, leaving their villages deserted; others received him with friendliness, and others warned him by fierce gestures and warlike demonstrations not to land. More than four hundred of the people at one place where they stopped came forward to meet them without arms and offering the hand. They allowed Gessi to fix a tent on their land to get a night of real repose, and gave him provisions of flour, sweet potatoes and chickens. At another place several people gathered to meet him with hostile intent, but a show of courage and some threats reduced them to such friendliness that the chief proposed the compact of blood with Gessi. As the friendship of this chief might be useful, he conquered his natural repugnance and resigned his arm to the ceremony.

The explorer counted on the shore here twenty-seven large and populous villages within two miles, the inhabitants of which were rich in cattle, grain and fruits. The river was here so wide that the opposite shore could scarcely be seen, and he found at last the canal leading to the lake.

Interminable equinoctial storms, when the rain fell in torrents as if the heavens were opened, delayed his progress. Cabrega, King of Unioro, who had his royal residence upon an island, hearing that their boats, which he called 'ships of war of the enemy,' were on the lake, ordered all the tribes on the shores to make war upon them. Therefore the warriors at the approach of Gessi gathered on the shore brandishing their lances, while all through the night the horn was sounded and fires were burning on the heights. They abandoned their cabins and sent the women and children with the cattle to the thick grass or the high mountains.

Nature was not less inhospitable than man, as the mountains came down to the shore in high precipices, and frequent hurricanes wetted them to the skin and filled the boats with water. While on this unfriendly shore Gessi was shipwrecked in a storm, but so near land that he and his crew swam to it, while the boat went under water. Their provisions and instruments were saved, indeed, but half ruined by the water, and when the storm ceased they were able to raise the boat and empty it of the sand in the bottom. It was almost impossible to find a place to anchor, as the shores were either sandy or filled with papyrus, and the harbours, where the natives landed easily with their light canoes, had too little water for the heavy iron boats of the expedition. About midway down the lake, however, he found an excellent port, which he recommends to future explorers as a place of refuge. The strong winds agitated the waters of the lake so that they once took refuge near a floating island containing thirty huts, from which the inhabitants fled at their approach, but returned after two hours. At another island, occupied by the people of Cabrega, Gessi, to escape the tempest on the lake, shot off a gun and landed in spite of their hostility. He told the timid not to fear the boats of the government, and recommended the hostile to submit.

Gessi was obliged not only to struggle with the elements and wild men and beasts, but with the men under his command, who, unaccustomed to navigating where the high waves often succeeded each other so fast that the boat filled with water in a moment, insisted on keeping close to the shore, where they were in much greater danger of shipwreck. In vain Gessi tried to persuade them of the greater security in deep water. They stood in a group, waiting resignedly for death and invoking the Prophet, until he, losing patience, beat one of them over the shoulders with all his strength. 'Why should we,' they said stolidly, 'oppose the will of God? If we are destined to be saved, we shall be.' But during a high tempest while in the middle of the lake they were persuaded that their boats would have been lost if near the shore. He passed three large cataracts and a river which empty into the lake, and found a village the people of which fled at first at their approach. But when Gessi, having killed a hippopotamus, advanced alone and unarmed, and with gestures offered them the carcase of the immense beast, they became friendly.

Slowly exploring thus the shores of the lake, and trying to discover from the natives all that they knew, the expedition arrived near the extremity. But the return was made in one night, when a hurricane drove them before the wind from one end of the lake to the other, and twenty miles out into the Nile.

'Never in my life,' says Gessi, 'was I in such danger on the water. The lake was furious, and we expected every moment to be swallowed up by the waves. It was impossible to land, as the mountains came down in precipices to the shore, and the waves beat there violently against the rocks.'

In thirty-five hours their boat ran 205 miles: 135 the length of the lake, 50 tacking to and fro, and 20 on the river.

Gessi had thus circumnavigated the lake, but had not, as he wished, ascended the rivers, approached the cataracts, or climbed the mountains on its shores. With a small escort of twelve soldiers he could not risk himself among those treacherous, hostile tribes, leaving the boats undefended. He discovered that the volume of water which Albert Nyanza furnishes the Nile comes from the cataracts seen by him, and from that of Murchison on the Victoria Nile. 'Whoever visits Lake Albert after me in the same season,' he says, 'and sees the floods of water which twenty times a day, and as often in the night, fall in rain, will not wonder at the volume of water that issues from it.'

After his return from this expedition Gessi made another, in company with Matteucci, leaving Khartoum, on the White Nile, and ascending the Blue Nile to Fadasi, whence they hoped to penetrate into Kaffa, and there meet Antinori, Cecchi, and Chiarini. The soul of the hero was expressed in few words as he set out from Khartoum: 'We shall meet hardships and sacrifices with tranquillity. If the journey were easy, it would not charm us.' But they were baffled by the hostility of the savages, and by the precipitous mountain roads, where camels and baggage could not pass. Within six days' march of Kaffa they were obliged, by the ferocity of the Amen-Niger, through whose land they must pass, to return. There was but one road to Kaffa, and these savages refused to let them advance. Persuasion and bribes had no effect, and finally, with the consciousness of having done their duty, they acknowledged that the expedition was impossible. Matteucci writes: 'You can imagine the state of mind of Gessi, who has never known fear, and always conquered with few and brave soldiers; here, near to the goal, and imprisoned by a swollen river, and with few fighting-men, he is like a wounded lion.'

If Romolo Gessi proved himself in this exploration a good sailor and brave explorer, he gave evidence also two years later, in the war against the slave-trade, of being a soldier and a leader. The evening before his departure he received the last instructions from Gordon, and next day, as he passed the governor's palace, saw him waving farewell from the balcony. Crowds of curious people gathered on the shore to see those whom they said Gordon was sending to certain death.

That same evening, as Gessi stood on deck, he saw a slave vessel slipping quietly past the steamer in the dark, and stopped it, liberating ninety-two blacks, who were packed close together, some of them chained, in the hold.

The vessel belonged to Ibrahim, the Governor-General of Central Africa, and was commanded by a relative of another high officer. This officer, Jussuf Bey, came next morning to beg for the release of the captain, but Gessi answered with scorn: 'Is this the loyalty with which you serve your sovereign and Gordon, who has given you the title of Bey, and whom you betray in this manner?' This man, his next in rank, would evidently give no aid in the difficult enterprise confided to him by Gordon.

The next day he met two slave ships, which immediately turned about for fear of him, and at the next landing sent all the slaves into the interior. At Fascioda he found an officer of the government, who, to increase his salary, engaged in the slave trade. The corruption was so general that none were found to betray the secrets of this horrible commerce. Even the Sultan of the Scilluk, the tribe from which the majority of the slaves were taken, finding it was to his interest to aid the stealers of human flesh, became a *negriero* against his own subjects. The Arabs of Khartoum found their richest harvest in this region, and year after year increased the trade, carrying away thousands of unfortunate creatures into slavery.

Gordon and Gessi, united in the saintly cause, made war upon this infamous commerce. Continuing up the Nile, Gessi met another steamer belonging to Ibrahim, upon which he found 170 slaves, 150 more having been sent on shore when he approached. He liberated these slaves, and wished to send them immediately to their homes, but the greater number were so weak and infirm that he could not do so for two or three days until they recovered strength.

All this so disgusted this brave, true man that he repented having accepted the mission. He retired to his cabin, giving orders not to be disturbed, and when alone felt tortured by a thousand anxieties for himself and for Gordon, involved in such a labyrinth. The officials employed by Gordon, many of whom he had advanced and loaded with favours, were almost without exception betraying him, and this *camorra* extended from the Upper Nile to Khartoum, and even to Cairo. Flourishing stations, founded by Gessi under Gordon's orders in 1875, and also native villages once rich and happy, had become desolate and ruined, and thorns and high grass had grown up in place of grain and fruits. The inhabitants were decimated, ill-treated or sent into slavery, and only undisciplined soldiers and Arab *gelabba*, or slave-dealers, were met with.

The first person who met Gessi at Ladò, where Emin Bey gave a festival for his arrival, was Ibrahim, who had already received the order from

Gordon to resign, and meanly implored the intervention of his accuser. Gordon, who had already used mildness in suppressing the slave-trade, empowered Gessi to be severe with the dealers when he got them in his power. The cruelties he saw there excited his pity for the blacks, and his indignation against their wicked persecutors. From Dem Ziber to Sciacca, twelve days' journey, there is no need of a guide, as the way is marked by skeletons of the blacks, most of whom are young boys and girls. Only thirty-five per cent. of those carried away from their homes reach Khartoum, dying along the road from lack of food, from fatigue, and exposure to heat and rain. Once, when Gessi found on the road a beautiful young girl whose throat had been cut to prevent her telling where the dealers had passed, he brought out thirty of these cruel *gelabba*, whom he held as prisoners, and ordered them to be shot in presence of one of the victims of their trade.

The question of the abolition of slavery is much more difficult than is generally believed in Europe. The right of possessing slaves being conceded by the Koran, the Arab, when told that leading his neighbour into slavery is the greatest crime a man can commit, answers, 'Why is it such a horrible thing? Has not God by means of Mahomet given us permission to possess slaves? Who can suppress the law of the Prophet? Who is superior to him?'

None, except the soldiers of the regular army, interested themselves in combatting Suleiman. Their interests would have suffered by his fall, and even Emin Bey considered the expedition of Gessi folly, with such a comparatively small force. With four companies of the regular army and 1000 soldiers, Gessi went forward, crossing rivers on flats made of cane, and struggling through a marsh where the thick mud was waist deep. After crossing this marsh forty-two persons were missing, having lost strength while in the mud, and preferring to die there rather than continue. The Italian hero himself confesses that 'It needs a character of iron to meet calmly all the obstacles in this country, which undermine the health of the strongest man.'

Gessi was reinforced by another thousand men, making his total number of troops 2400. Among the newly arrived was a white man from Niam-Niam of the West, whose relatives, except one brother, were all black. He was not an albino, but was surprisingly white; his face rosy, his hair red, and his eyes blue. Miani also has reported having seen among the Niam-Niam of the West white men who were not albinos.

From fear of Suleiman or jealousy of Gessi's success, the troops and ammunition he expected were not always sent to him, even in his greatest need, thus increasing his peril and strengthening the enemy.

Gessi's compassion for the poor negroes was constantly excited by the sight of their misery. In one of his expeditions in search of Suleiman he was met by three sheikhs who wished to speak to him. He alighted from his horse, and under the shade of a magnificent tamarind tree gave them the audience they desired. The oldest said, 'We are the sheikhs of the villages Bisellia, Bongo and Gonfora. Suleiman has captured our wives and daughters, and destroyed our substance, so that for months we live like beasts in the high grass. We have come to tell you that we and all our men are ready to aid you as far as we can. Command, and we will obey.' One of them, who had a sweet expression of countenance, then took out from his bag made of skin a little pot of honey, and offered it weeping, saying, 'I thought I would bring you this; we possess nothing else.' The old sheikh accompanied Gessi for a time, and one day presented his seven sons, saying, 'Here are all my sons. They have no weapons, as Suleiman has taken them, but you will arm them, and they will die for this good cause.' Four of these sons in fact were killed in the various battles.

At another place the natives ran to meet him, gesticulating so as to show there had been some misfortune. Fifteen armed Arabs had captured 150 of the tribe, and carried them away chained to Suleiman. Gessi immediately sent 100 soldiers after them, liberated the negroes and sent them back to their families.

Suleiman, with 11,000 men, attacked the government troops at Dem Idris, and was driven back with the loss of 4000. This unexpected defeat was soon known in all Bar-Ghasal, but the Arabs believed that Suleiman would finally conquer. He returned and bombarded the camp of Gessi at Wau, killing many natives, 5000 of whom had taken refuge there to avoid being captured as slaves.

Finally, after many battles and skirmishes, Gessi with 250 soldiers surrounded Suleiman with 1600 by night, captured, and next day shot him and nine of his generals.

Through all the seven years spent in Equatorial Soudan, Gessi expressed the utmost reverence and affection for General Gordon. His letters, published from time to time in the *Bulletin* of the Commercial Exploration Society of Milan, have recently been collected by his only son, Felice Gessi, and dedicated to the *Santa Memoria di C. E. Gordon-Pascià*.

For his services here and victories over Suleiman, the slave-dealer, and the Arab rebels, he was made general, and Governor of Equatorial Africa. Suleiman had a force of 23,000 well-armed men, but the superior military genius of Gessi conquered with a small army of 3300 men. Gessi calculated that Suleiman alone carried away from Bar-Ghasal 50,000 slaves annually, and that not less than 100,000 were captured in all yearly.

The Italian soldier and explorer exclaims, 'My greatest reward is to have liberated Africa from Suleiman, and saved the poor negroes. I have armed them, so that they can defend themselves.' But, recalled by the jealousy of the Arab merchants of Khartoum, to whom this trade is profitable, he left Bar-Ghasal on board the ship Safia, with five hundred followers, and was over three months entangled in the gigantic vegetation of the river, which stops navigation as effectually as the ice in northern regions. Rebellion and famine tortured him on this tragic journey, the sufferings of which finally cost his life. The *sudd* or mass of enwoven plants, a tangled skein sometimes 12,000 feet in length, was a formidable impediment. All the efforts of Gessi to free the Safia, which was not strong enough to force its way through, were unavailing. The men worked with hatchets and spades, but the vessel made no progress, and the horrors of famine were soon added to fever and distress.

The bodies of the women and children, the weak and the old, who first died, lay putrefying for weeks on the strong branches of the dreadful plants that held the vessel in a giant embrace. Several of the dead bodies were devoured by the survivors, the moral effect of these horrors being greater upon Gessi than his sufferings from want of food. The people cut up the skins in which their effects were wrapped, soaked the strips in water over night, and then boiled them to eat. Many of the sufferers walked the deck all night, tormented by mosquitos, and sometimes treading on the sleepers, when groans, screams, and fighting ensued. Help came at last from Khartoum, Marno, the friend of Gessi, having cut through the *sudd* and rescued him when death seemed certain. Gessi, reduced to a skeleton, was lifted like a child upon the other vessel, but a fever ensued, which soon after ended his life at Suez.

The journal he kept was sent to the Roman Geographical Society. The night before the rescuing vessel came he wrote: 'I felt myself dying. I felt languor and heaviness, and my strength was leaving me. I had escaped death in so many battles, and yet must die at last in the middle of a river. We are constantly labouring at one plant 12,000 feet long. The people are half immersed in water, and we are surrounded as if by a strong wall. We can go neither backward nor forward, nor even send messengers for relief, as both the shores are populated by warlike and savage enemies.' At the end of the second month he had written: 'There is no hope of salvation. All begin to abandon themselves to desperation, and, seated on deck with their heads down, wait for death.' On the last day of December he wrote: 'This is the most terrible day. To-morrow is the new year— a sad day for me. I think of my home, of my wife, my children, who in their play know nothing of the terrible condition of their father. So ends the year 1880, and I am reduced to this extremity because I was too fortunate in my campaign against slavery.'

But on the 5th of January they hear guns and see the vapour from a steamer. 'It is the Ismailia! Great God be thanked!' Tears fall from all their eyes, and the lion-hearted Gessi himself weeps as these suffering creatures go up one after another to kiss his hands and feet. 'God be thanked! We are safe!'

PELLEGRINO MATTEUCCI.

CHAPTER V.

DOCTOR PELLEGRINO MATTEUCCI.

Doctor Pellegrino Matteucci was the companion of Gessi's unsuccessful journey up the Blue Nile towards Kaffa. He made another expedition with Bianchi into Abyssinia, and finally immortalised his name by the famous journey across the continent from the Red Sea to the mouth of the Niger. This was one of the boldest and most important journeys yet accomplished in Africa, but a violent malarial fever contracted there terminated his brilliant career in London, while on his way home to Italy.

The letters of Matteucci on his first expedition are eloquent and copious records of the strange scenes and curious customs of African life, his vivid imagination revelling in the wild and romantic scenery through which he passed. He describes the desert from Cairo to Khartoum as 'space lost in the distant horizon. Here there is not a square inch of shade, not a blade of grass, not the possibility of finding a drop of water. The yellow sand makes a strange contrast with the whitened bones of thousands and thousands of camels, which have been the food of hyenas inhabiting the desert.'

Almost the only flower near the springs of the oasis is the Nilotic acacia, which diffuses rich fragrance in the air. The safety enjoyed in the desert is phenomenal, as the Bedouins, instead of being, as they are often described, robbers and assassins, are as proud of their honesty as of their independence.

Once, on the Nile, going up to the region whence they intended to travel by land towards Kaffa, they raised the Italian banner on the vessel to please the Arab captain; but the rattling of heavy chains below called their attention to a young girl, an Abyssinian slave, who was condemned to receive two hundred blows. Matteucci and Gessi told the captain that the Italian flag should never wave over such cruelty, and thus obtained the release of the girl, who returned to her duties with a smiling face.

The defeat of the expedition to Kaffa was a bitter disappointment, but Matteucci went the next year to Abyssinia with Bianchi, both being sent there by the African Commercial Society of Milan. He observed everything, the patriotic thought for

Italy being supreme in his mind. 'I do not seek,' he says, 'easily bought praise, but care only for the interests and the future of my country, and to increase the love for geographical studies in Italy, most happy if this should be with the sacrifice of my own life.'

He had already paid tribute to the malarious climate of the White Nile with four fevers, but on his return from Abyssinia plunged again into the unknown darkness of the African continent.

The last journey of Matteucci, commenced with Lieutenant Massari and Prince Giovanni Borghese, was from the Red Sea to the Atlantic Ocean. The youngest son of the Borghese family of Rome bore the expenses of this expedition, and himself went as far as Wadai, killing a lion on the way, and bearing himself like a true explorer, but there reluctantly yielded to the wishes of his family and returned. Matteucci and Massari left the fantastic minarets and shady palm groves of Khartoum and El-Obeid behind, and travelling on camels at night, when the siren of African scenery presented itself with the most lovely aspect, over thirsty plains, though sometimes attacked by savages, traversed the kingdoms of Wadai, Bornu, Kano, and Nupe. Their journey, which crossed Africa diagonally, traversing thirty meridians and parallels, was believed impossible at Cairo.

The tribes here fear the Turkish and Egyptian power, and with reluctance permit the entrance into their territory of any white man—as to them all men not black are Turks or Egyptians. Matteucci and Massari went as pilgrims with no show of wealth, but they persuaded the Sultan of Wadai that the King of Italy would avenge their death if they were not protected, and would make presents if they were.

They saved the lives of 400 prisoners of war by telling the sultan that he could make no more acceptable present to the King of Italy than by sparing them. In Bornu they found an Italian who had been a slave there for nineteen years, having been left behind by Nachtigal. Valpreda reluctantly let them depart, and fell weeping on their necks, but was consoled by the promise that they would send for him. When the travellers reached the English settlements at the mouth of the Niger they were received with kindness and sent in a vessel to London. But Matteucci was destined never again to see his 'dear' Bologna, and the inanimate body was brought home by Massari, and buried with great honour.

The thought of Bologna pursued Matteucci in that journey across the African continent. Every anniversary, when he remembered that his family and friends were meeting together, was torture to him. Night and day he thought of them, and seemed to have a sad presentiment that he should never see them again. He died at thirty-one years of age, too soon to gather up and make use of the fruits of his last journey.

Matteucci was born in Ravenna in 1850, but was carried by his parents to Bologna when two years old. After taking the regular course at the University of Rome, he studied medicine and the Arabic language, in order to prepare himself for life in Africa in the service of the Roman Catholic missions. This had been his settled purpose from boyhood, and this induced him to study medicine instead of law, as his father desired. The occupation of Rome by the Italian army in 1870 interrupted his study of medicine, but he continued it in Ravenna. When the Geographical Society of Rome sent out its first company of explorers to Africa in 1876, Matteucci was disappointed at not being included.

But Romolo Gessi, just returned from the circumnavigation of Lake Albert, invited him to join another expedition, the object of which was to reach Kaffa, not through Shoa, but up the Blue Nile, by the way of Fazoglu and Fadasi. The history of this journey was written by Matteucci in a book called *Soudan and Galla*, published soon after his return. The Society for Commercial Explorations in Africa, founded at Milan, then selected him as the head of an expedition to Abyssinia, which he accomplished in less than one year, and soon after published another book, entitled *In Abyssinia*.

These two journeys were only preliminary to another which he proposed making in Wadai, or Central Soudan, and he soon found means to accomplish his purpose. The offer was made to him by the commercial house of Arbib, to accompany as physician one of the caravans which they sent annually from Tripoli to Wadai. He could return either by the Egyptian provinces or by Tripoli.

The grand idea of crossing the African continent

from the Red Sea to the Atlantic had not yet occurred to him. But while at Cairo making this arrangement he met a young Roman noble, Giovanni Borghese, who proposed paying all the expenses of a hunting expedition to the African provinces adjoining Wadai. The sum offered was more than enough, Matteucci thought, to reach Dar-Fur and Kordovan, and might be sufficient to penetrate farther into the heart of Africa. He had learned in his previous journeys that the surest plan of travelling in those unknown regions, was not to carry much baggage, which was often left along the way, but to do without many things usually considered necessary.

The Geographical Society of Rome, and also the Ministry of Agriculture, gave money to aid the expedition, while the Ministry of the Marine sent with Matteucci and Borghese a brave young naval officer, Lieutenant Alfonso Maria Massari. They left Cairo for Suez, and at Suakin on the Red Sea landed, to cross the desert to Khartoum. After Borghese left them on the confines of Wadai, Matteucci and Massari, conquering the reluctance of the Sultan of Wadai to receive travellers from the Egyptian provinces, remained there forty-nine days. Here their plan of returning to Europe by way of Tripoli was changed, as they would have been obliged to wait eight months in Wadai for a caravan, and the sultan absolutely refused them permission to return by that way. It was fortunate not only for their fame, but also for their safety, as at that time all of Northern Sahara was disturbed by religious wars, which would have made it dangerous for Christians to travel there. Central Soudan was free from that agitation, and having reached Bornu they were nearer the Gulf of Guinea than the Mediterranean.

This brilliant exploration was made, therefore, without a previous definite plan, and as Matteucci was part of the time a prisoner on the way, and suffered from inflammation of the eyes and the African fever, he left few notes and letters.

Massari on his return gave several lectures before the Royal Geographical Society, but the ready and eloquent descriptions of Matteucci were silenced by death. Only a short diary with a few notes for each day remains, a pathetic proof of the hardships of the journey. The absence of all news from his friends in Europe was severely felt by this enthusiastic traveller, whose motive for exposing himself to those dangers was not gain, or even scientific investigation, but fame and the approbation of those he knew. From the confines of Wadai to Bornu the travellers were isolated, and the way before them was unknown and uncertain. The brief notes in his diary at this time prove how dark a cloud of fear and uncertainty had settled upon them. The Sultan of Wadai was known to be perfidious and cruel, having before murdered another explorer named Vogel. He kept them waiting as prisoners 113 days before permitting them to enter his kingdom, and treated them as suspicious characters. The European was always to him a spy, and he could not understand what motive induced him to undertake the long and dangerous journey.

The time occupied by Matteucci in going from Cairo to Accasa, at the mouth of the Niger, was sixteen months and a half, eight of which were spent in involuntary halts, when they were waiting the pleasure of the various petty sovereigns on the way. They went from Khartoum to Accasa, a distance of 3000 miles, at an average of fourteen miles a day. This, in Africa, with all the material difficulties of the way for living and defence, the slowness of the drivers and servants, the few hours left for travel by sun and rain, is a remarkable instance of swift travelling.

Although the last diary of Matteucci is meagre, and very different in its short notes from the eloquent descriptions he gave of his former journeys, there is enough to give an idea of the beauty of the way and the sorrows they endured. In Dar-Tama he says, 'We see that we have left the dominions of Egypt. The villages are numerous, and inhabited by a tall people who dress neatly and show much respect to their chiefs. The Sultan Idris being with us, they did not run away, as they would have done if we had been alone, but gave us beer and chickens. Before entering the city of Gneri, the residence of Sultan Ibrahim, we rested an hour to prepare for a triumphant ingress. Fifty cavaliers with long lances and many-coloured dresses came out to meet us with trumpets, and amused themselves by making a feigned attack and by races. The "city" of Gneri consists of 300 huts made of straw, except those of Ibrahim and his son, which are made of earth.'

The sultan received them with great ceremony, making an exception to his rule of never seeing or speaking directly with strangers. He questioned them closely as to their plans, and gave them a friendly letter to the Sultan of Wadai, which he sent with theirs by one of his own servants. But Sultan Jussuf of Wadai kept them waiting for months at the confines of his kingdom, and sent messengers to inquire of his old friend Ibrahim 'who these Christians were, and what was their real object in making the journey.' They came, he said, from an enemy's country, Dar-Fur, and his messengers must examine them and decide whether they were really Europeans, or came only from Cairo. The only place in Europe of which they had heard was Malta, but that served to convince them that Matteucci and Massari were true men, and they were permitted at last to enter the unexplored land of Wadai.

But although this was the object of their journey, they did not leave Tama and Sultan Idris without forebodings. Borghese left them at Gneri, and Sultan Idris followed them five hours to the border of Wadai, and took leave with an embrace and tears. The heat was intense, Matteucci suffered from inflammation of the eyes, and when they reached Abescer, the capital, every living thing seemed to have fled. A terrible uncertainty weighed upon them. Even the sultan had abandoned the city, and although he provided them with food, it was evident that they were prisoners. Finally they were told that he would receive them, and accept the gifts sent to him by the King of

Italy. On examining their valuables they realised that they were truly in a land of robbers, and longed to escape to Bornu. But they prepared for the momentous visit and, dressed in white and carrying the gifts, entered the palace, passing through two lines of slaves, and reached at last the place where the sultan was hidden behind a closed curtain. The unseen individual, who they afterwards learned was not the sultan, asked them many questions, and promised to send them on to Bornu, from whence they could return to their own home.

They afterwards received the sultan's gifts— black and white ostrich feathers for the king, and for them four servants and three camels—and finally were permitted to leave Abescer, where, in fact, a plot against their lives had been made, but was not carried into effect.

These were the saddest days of the journey, and the thoughts of Matteucci constantly returned to his *cara Bologna*. They traversed an immense desert plain, where there are no representatives of the animal kingdom, and only two wells in twenty-four miles, and after reaching a town in a more fertile district, made a halt of several days against their will. 'We have stopped, but I do not know why,' is a frequent note in the sad diary.

The road is always over the desert, an infinite reach of level plain, the earth tinted red, a bronze sky above their heads, and an atmosphere of fire. They pass small villages now and then, where there are wells and a few palm trees, but at last reach a better land with luxuriant vegetation. The road here is wide and beautiful ; flocks and herds abound ; there are 'many sycamores, beautiful women, excellent men and populous villages.'

They visit the sultan of another small kingdom called Midogo, who receives them kindly and invites them to return. On their second visit this *simpatico sultano* asks them secretly for poison, which Matteucci promises, but gives him the next day a package of quinine. Thus alternately between the silence and poverty of the desert and the miracles of African vegetation, between rapid marches and mysterious halts, sick with fever, lame, robbed of their goods and even of their camels, they are passed on from one jealous, cruel and suspicious sultan to another.

Bornu is a populous region, with fine scenery, its capital, Cuca, situated upon a lake ; Kano, the capital of Socotto, is a large city well built with two-storey houses, and having a bazaar, where all the products of the country are sold. The Sultan of Nupe received them dressed in magnificent robes of velvet and satin, and gave them a beautiful leopard skin. He was the last of the sultans who had tormented them for months, and they left his capital, Bidda, near the Niger, with joy. The hardships of the journey were ended, and in a boat they reached Acassa, at the mouth of the Niger, there taking the steamer which conveyed them to London, where, as already stated, Matteucci died.

ORAZIO ANTINORI.

CHAPTER VI.

ORAZIO ANTINORI AND HIS COMPANIONS.

BESIDES Miani, Piaggia, Gessi, and Matteucci, there is a company of explorers, the chief of whom was Marquis Antinori, the brave old man who dedicated the last years of his life to founding an Italian station in Shoa. He was sent by the Roman Geographical Society in 1875, his companions at various times being Chiarini, Cecchi, Martini, Bianchi, and Antonelli. The grand idea of the society was to form a depôt of supplies and relief in the Shoa, from which the hardy explorers might push onward to the equatorial lakes and discover the secrets of that vast unexplored region, twice as large as Italy, between Abyssinia and Lake Victoria.

The project was received enthusiastically, and large sums of money were subscribed. Antinori, then sixty-five years of age, was selected as the chief of the expedition, and Chiarini and Martini were his first companions, the others being added afterwards.

The results of this effort have been inferior to the anticipations, yet a flourishing station now exists in Africa; the region has been thoroughly studied, and the Italian influence prevails there. None of the explorers penetrated the inhospitable region between the Italian station and the lakes, and their ambitious hopes were disappointed.

Antinori died in 1882, at the station Let-Marefià; Chiarini died while a prisoner to the savage Queen of Ghèra, and Cecchi, after incredible sufferings, escaped from that terrible prison-house.

The journey of Antinori and his companions from Zeila on the Red Sea to Liccè, the residence of the half savage King Menilek, who gave them land for a station, was dangerous and difficult. They were often obliged to shoot animals for sustenance; sometimes there was no trace of vegetation, and the savages they saw were half nude and armed with lances, while their servants robbed them when it was possible. Where the rivers were swollen they crossed by swimming, often losing their effects, and having their barometers and watches ruined by the water.

But these discomforts were forgotten in the splendour of the reception given them on their arrival by King Menilek. Four hundred horsemen came out to meet them, preceded by fantastic music, while two caparisoned mules were sent for Antinori and Chiarini. An immense crowd of negroes and Arabs had gathered to witness this triumphal entry, and the booming of the sole cannon owned by Menilek added warlike glory to the occasion. Menilek, surrounded by his princes, and by Monsignor Massaia, the bishop,

MENILEK.

who lived in the Shoa thirty years, received them, and asked with infantile greed and curiosity for the gifts sent by the King of Italy. Menilek— 'King of kings and conqueror of the Lion of the tribe of Judah'—is a fine-looking young man, with black hair and beard, a frank expression; is a great friend of Europeans, and eager to possess arms the mechanism of which he understands.

The natural beauties of the Shoa, the delightful

climate and fertility of the soil, are dwelt upon by Antinori with the enthusiasm of youth.

It is there a perpetual spring; the roses and jasmines, the acacias and mimosas, the bananas, cotton plants, sugar-canes, and lemons, the grain, lentils, beans and peas, the mint and sage, the wild olives and monstrous sycamores; the monkeys, with silvery white tales and black coats; the birds, with green bodies and red wings, or yellow bodies and black heads, charm him;—and he writes long letters home with his left hand, the right having been rendered useless by a wound received in the chase.

Menilek granted Antinori thirty or forty acres of land situated on the side of a hill in a kind of delta formed by two torrents that met at its base. The harvests on this fertile soil are gathered three times a year, and Antinori found ample subsistence for the explorers and forty Abyssinian servants, whom he gradually gathered around him. Let-Marefià is a bit of Italy in Africa, where the Italian banner still waves. The explorers studied the animals and flowers, the insects, the soil, the people of the land, and soon collected specimens that filled thirty cases. With these proofs of their skill and industry, and also to procure supplies, Martini returned to Italy. Not less than thirty-four days were required to reach Zeila, there being no road, and the tribes often hostile or thieving.

The duty of Martini, aided later by Cecchi, Bianchi, Antonelli, and Giulietti, to carry the coveted gifts from Zeila to Liceè, was not an easy one. The way lay through dense forests, over desert plains, and unbridged rivers, or in the pebbly beds of dry summer torrents; while the idle character of the natives, their lying, thieving, and wars, as well as the dreadful epidemics to which they are subject, added to the difficulties in communicating with Italy. One or even two years sometimes passed without news from Antinori's isolated station, an Arab messenger often keeping a letter by him without thinking that haste was necessary. Caravans of 300 camels leave Liccè once a year, carrying ivory, coffee, wax, skins, spices, and feathers.

We can imagine Antinori settled in the beautiful home at Let-Marefià. The grounds are watered by perennial streams, and adorned with lovely vegetation, and a gigantic sycamore growing on one side served for shade as well as to attract birds for Antinori's collections. The old hero confesses that after all his journeyings he longed to return to Italy, but yet continued his indefatigable labours, and was determined also to accompany Chiarini and Cecchi towards Kaffa and the lakes. In fact, he began the journey with them, but the younger men persuaded him, on account of his mutilated hand, to return.

Antinori says, 'Cecchi, with tears in his eyes, threw his arms about my neck, and Chiarini did the same, imploring me not to proceed, and I, sadly kissing them on their foreheads, left them almost without a word.' It was a final parting with Chiarini, who never returned.

Left alone at Let-Marefià the Marquis Antinori

made excursions into the southern provinces near Shoa. In the country of the Ada-Galla he discovered two small lakes, in addition to the six others already known, and continued also to make his collections of birds and insects. Although suffering from his constant labours, from solitude and the gradual advance of old age, he could not resist the temptation to accompany King Menilek in a campaign against the tribes on Lake Zuai. He hoped to explore the vicinity of that lake, as yet unvisited by Italians, but a series of disasters, bad weather and great fatigue injured his health so much that he returned to Let-Marefià, anxious at last to get back to Italy before he died.

But this consolation was denied him, since, obliged to wait from March to August, until the summer rains were over, he grew worse, and died on August 22, 1882. He was buried at Let-Marefià under the sycamore which he loved, and over his grave was erected a little hut, which is kept in order by the servants of the establishment, now under the care of Dr. Ragazzi and Dr. Traversi. When the sad news reached Italy, a memorial service was held in his native city Perugia, and Cecchi was there.

Although not thirty years of age at this time, Cecchi was already grey and wrinkled from the terrible privations suffered during the five years spent in weary marches over torrid plains; in climbing precipitous mountains or swimming wide and turbid rivers; in anxious days with robber bands of savages; in fevers, imprisonment, and slavery.

The story this bold mariner of the Adriatic told

to the Geographical Society of Rome on his return brought tears to all eyes. The account of his first journey in 1877 from Zeila to Let-Marefià to carry supplies to Antinori proves what marvellous courage and patience were needed by these travellers in the midst of a ferocious and suspicious people.

A presentiment of future subjugation makes these Africans hostile to strangers. 'I know the art of these people,' said the Negus Theodore of Ethiopia. 'They send first merchants and missionaries, then ambassadors, and at last cannon. It is better for us to begin with the cannon.'

The dangers and privations of the way over the desert to Shoa are greatly diminished, as the inhabitants are now convinced that commerce with Europeans is to their interest. But in 1877, when Cecchi and Martini made the second expedition there, the journey was difficult. Being ready to start at the middle of May, they began to load 120 camels with their baggage, which consisted of 164 strong boxes well lined within and varnished on the outside. Besides these they had baskets full of charcoal, to light the fires for their cooking along the way: a quantity of curtains and poles for tents; sixty bales of white and coloured muslin, and many other bundles containing rice, tobacco, ropes, Venetian beads, and lead. Sixty men to load the camels, the drivers, and the keepers of the mules and camels formed an undisciplined, noisy, riotous little army, which was long in reducing itself to a caravan. The scene to Cecchi, who was ignorant of the customs of the country, seemed a riot, and he expected to see his baggage used as projectiles by the noisy mob. The young camels which had never been loaded before added to the general confusion. They refused to kneel, tore the rope from the driver's hand, and with the load ill-balanced and all on one side trotted off among the others, frightening them all. It was laughable to see one which had run away brought back, forced to kneel and receive the load, and then with one of its fore-feet tied up, jump about in every grotesque attitude.

Padre Alexis, a priest who was going to Abyssinia, joined them with twelve camels; and some merchants with another addition made the caravan consist of 200 camels, which, marching in single file at equal distances from each other, covered a space one mile and a half long. At the earliest dawn of day the caravan begins its slow march over the desert, following the leader, who sings a low monotonous song. The camels measure their walk by this song, hastening or going slower according to its melody, and when it ceases bending the knee and waiting patiently in the sand to be relieved of their load. The caravan seems a village in motion, every worldly possession on the backs of the camels, and the scenes of family life that are usually shut up within walls enacted under the open sky. This is the free life of the desert which has charmed more than one Italian traveller. The trammels of our civilization seem to weigh heavily on those who have imbibed this love for the immense majestic solitude, where man feels at once his own insignificance and his own importance as the lord of Nature.

The heat grew insupportable and the tents were like furnaces; so that they were obliged to travel at night, when there was a fresh soft breeze. They reached a station called Ugas-Robli, after the name of the chief, according to the fashion in this part of Africa. This inconvenient custom of calling not only the village but the inhabitants after the chief, makes confusion for the traveller, who, when he returns, finds another chief and another name.

Water began to be scarce, and Cecchi and Martini suffered from thirst, but on the sixth day they reached Danan, where the inhabitants of the Somali race surrounded them, curious to view such rare animals as these. The Somali of the coast are believed to be of Arabic origin, their ancestors having at different periods crossed the Gulf of Aden and landed at Cape Guardafui. In course of time they have become a mixed race, and now have many features in common with the Galla, the Afar, and the other tribes inhabiting that region. Like the Galla, they are good horsemen, and can throw a lance and catch it again while in motion. They chase the elephant, the lion, the leopard, antelope, zebra, and ostrich. If they promise friendship to a stranger, he is considered a member of the family, and the Abbà, or Father, is his protector. All of the family of the Abbà must perish before the stranger is abandoned. The Somali of the coast being generally merchants, camel drivers, and porters, have fixed dwelling-places, but those of the interior are wanderers, owing to the scarcity of water and vegetation.

They move about from place to place seeking pasture for their flocks.

Cecchi and Martini watched by turns during the night, often shooting off a gun to drive away the Isa-Somali, and let them know that some one was awake. These brigands of the desert came around them in the morning armed with clubs and knives, demanding rice, tobacco, and dates. But they fled precipitately when Cecchi, Martini, and four of the servants presented their guns and bayonets, believing that if six persons would dare to confront 200 they must have some miraculous weapons of defence. Padre Alexis defended himself with a crucifix, having faith that it would defend him even better than guns.

They travelled for days in the narrow dry bed of a torrent between two long chains of volcanic mountains where the vegetation was scarce. The Isa-Somali again surrounded them, begging for their goods, and were driven away by another warlike demonstration. Four times along this route the travellers were obliged to leave behind part of their baggage, on account of the weakness or illness of the camels, and the Isa-Somali fixed covetous eyes on the remainder—the muslin and beads which they were using every effort to preserve, as these took the place of money. After eleven days of dusty and thirsty travel they found for the first time running water and trees.

Martini went out with his gun and returned in a few moments with a gazelle and an otter, the meat of which, with fresh water and a cool night, strengthened them for the long journey over the hot plain before them. Here the camel, the ship of the desert, hastened its step, seeing here and there along the way so many skeletons of its race.

Cecchi, who had stopped a few moments to take observations, was surprised here by an optical phenomenon, which caused him to bestride his mule in hot haste to overtake the caravan. The *fata morgana* showed him the caravan, as he thought, two or three miles away, part of it reduced to microscopical proportions, and part grown to colossal size, moving slowly in the air over a stratum of shining silver. Almost despairing of reaching it, Cecchi found himself in a moment breathless and alarmed, galloping beside his companions.

The water at the next station was so bitter that, thirsty as they were, it was hard to drink it; and yet before reaching the Oasis of Arrò this bitter water, which in addition had grown rancid and nauseating from the butter spread on the inside of the goat-skin that held it, saved them from great suffering. Water was abundant at Arrò, and they were tempted to encamp in a forest watered all the year round by a torrent. But the leader of the caravan advised them to occupy an elevated position at some distance, where they were less liable to be surrounded and annoyed by the Somali, who live here, and possess numerous herds of camels, cows, and goats. The precaution did not preserve them from annoyance, as in half an hour 500 Somali came out of the forest around their tents to watch them. Seated on the handles of their lances, which they fixed in the earth, these savages followed every movement of Cecchi and Martini. Now and then one more courageous than the rest entered their tents, and covering nose and mouth with a cloth to avoid the smell which, according to them, emanates from white men, examined every article. They saw no use in the greater part of the possessions of the strangers, and considered their mode of walking and sitting, the colour of their skin, their language as surprising and ridiculous. They frightened the women who ventured to touch the white men's clothes, or anything in the tents, by saying that they were dangerous animals, even capable of eating women alive.

Dangers and difficulties of all kinds increased on the way. A hurricane one night carried their tents three miles away, hyenas assailed them; and they received the compliments of the robber chief Ugas-Robli, which meant either tribute or war. Martini used every art of persuasion he possessed, apostrophising the camel drivers with fierce and eloquent words and gestures, and urging them to move on to the next station secretly by night. As they were nearly all subjects of the Sultan Ugas-Robli, and had left their families and flocks in his power, they refused. Martini only succeeded with his passionate gestures in amusing 500 Somali, who, seated on their lances in a circle, enjoyed this to them interesting and original representation.

The caravan waited while Martini and Cecchi, to calm their wrath, went into the beautiful forest with their guns, killing to the wonder of their Somali guides a boar, several hares, and some guinea hens in a few minutes. They found their tents on their return surrounded by 2000 Somali armed to the teeth, to whom were added the day after several hundred more accompanying the sultan. The forest seemed filled by magic with thousands of black heads moving in and out among the thick foliage and the vapours arising from the river. The sultan exacted a heavy tribute, and after receiving it tried to assail them treacherously by night with his 2000 Somali, but was repulsed.

At Tull-Harrè, where there is a forest and a stream of clear water, they sent back the Somali guides and drivers, and fell into the hands of Mohammed-Bali, of the Afar race, who, expert and malignant, made the rest of their journey even more unhappy and unfortunate than the first part. The Somali were gone, and the Afar men refused to help them; mosquitos by night, and the heat by day were unbearable; and reptiles and hyenas disturbed their sleep.

Cecchi, who one night had taken his bed outside the tent and covered it with a hide well tucked in around, to preserve him from the unwelcome company of reptiles, was awakened by a chorus of howls, and found himself and his bed being dragged away. A troop of hyenas, attracted by the odour of rancid butter with which the hide had been dressed, entered the camp while all were asleep, and gathering around Cecchi's bed contested for the prize. They were easily frightened away by the explosion of his pistol, as they are generally afraid of living beings, preferring dead bodies. They were bold enough for this feat, however, and afterwards took a leather pillow from under the head of a camel-driver, and gathered round the camp at night to possess themselves of the carcases of the dead camels.

Soon after this the explorers had an experience of savage warfare, in which they were compelled to take part to defend the traitorous and thieving Afars who had them in charge. For days they had been waiting, using up their small stock of provisions in the meanwhile, for the Afars to reduce their demands of payment, and had gone out in the woods to hunt, when they were alarmed by desperate cries of 'the Assaimara! the Assaimara.' Herds of cattle came running towards them as if for protection, and women passed, weeping as they went, laden with their domestic goods and their children. The Afars implored them to take part in the battle, which, considering they were in the power of these robbers, they finally did, routing the enemy by the mere sight of their guns. Even after this victory the Afars refused to guide them towards Shoa, and they were in danger of losing all when near their destination. Martini prepared to go alone to Shoa to ask help from King Menilek, but letters reached them informing him of the death of his mother, which so afflicted him that he was unable to exert himself.

Padre Alexis, who, from having prayed often bareheaded in the sun, had been ill, resolved, sick as he was, to try to reach Shoa, and left them. Finally, after forty days spent in that place, the

Afar leader, Mohammed-Bali, consented to move on; and it was full time, for the rainy season was near, their provisions were exhausted, and the small-pox, which decimated the inhabitants of the country, attacked some of their servants. At the first station they found Padre Alexis sick and starving, whom they took back to their caravan and nursed with every attention until his death some time later.

Padre Alexis, like Cecchi and Martini, had no more camels to advance with, and no money to hire others, so that he was obliged to burn part of his baggage. This order he gave to two negroes, ex-slaves, who had been educated at a missionary college in France, but who, instead of becoming honest men, were, according to Cecchi, 'ungrateful, liars, thieves, dissolute, cowards, and traitors.' Instead of destroying the useless baggage, they opened several boxes containing rich vestments of the Roman Church which Padre Alexis was carrying to Abyssinia. In a moment the Afars gathered howling around, decking themselves in all that finery. The women, who when young are beautiful and have forms like Greek statues, put on the rich sacerdotal cloaks, and with the greasy goat-skin pitcher on their shoulder went down to the river to draw water. Some tied altar cloths around their waists, some put stoles around their necks, or surplices trimmed with lace over their own greasy shirts, and all without exception ornamented their necks and breasts with medals, rosaries, and crosses. When Cecchi, moved by the desperate prayers of Padre Alexis, tried to catch them they bounded away like gazelles, making the sacred vestments fly about in a ridiculous manner.

Difficulties increased, their camels were reduced in number from 160 to 24; the way was monotonous and squalid; the people among whom they passed generally hostile; water scarce and very bad, until they reached a small lake. Then the road began to ascend to the high plains of Abyssinia, which rises in three terraces like a rock between Soudan and the desert on the Red Sea. The river Huash, 130 feet wide, with a rapid current and filled with crocodiles, seemed an insurmountable obstacle, as the Afars refused to help them cross it. Cecchi at length swam across, fastened a rope to a tree, returned hand over hand on the rope, made a flat boat of wooden boxes, on which they placed their valuable goods, and without help from the natives, to their great wonder succeeded in crossing the formidable river.

A few more days of fatiguing travel, new encounters with elephants and leopards, hyenas, and crocodiles, and annoyances of all kinds from the thieving Afars, brought them almost to despair. An immense python, near whose den Cecchi's servant Lorenzo had established the kitchen, departed one day in a very bad humour, upsetting the plates, pots, and kettles. Padre Alexis died here in great agony, and was buried by Cecchi, Martini having left to seek the road to Shoa, and to find help. But before his return a numerous party of Abyssinians sent by Menilek, who had heard that a white man was wandering alone in the dangerous Afar country, reached Cecchi. Cecchi's joy was so great at seeing these messengers that he says ' he could have kissed them if they had not been so dirty.' Martini also was found, and the travellers, after more than four months, reached Farè, where they met King Menilek and their friends, Antinori and Chiarini.

QUEEN OF SHOA.

CHAPTER VII.

CECCHI AND CHIARINI AMONG THE EQUATORIAL LAKES.

BUT for Cecchi and Chiarini, Let-Marefià was only a stopping-place and a base of supplies, as their aim was to explore the unknown region between Shoa and the equatorial lakes. This region, occupied by many different tribes, all either enemies or unknown to Menilek, their protector, is a land of tropical vegetation, where the roads are often impassable, mountainous, and intersected with rivers that in the rainy season are swollen and difficult to cross. They left the delightful climate of Shoa and the comparative comfort of Let-Marefià with a small armed escort of hunters and servants. The country before them was new, and charmed them onward with the hope of making some discoveries. Even in the delirium of the fevers which they contracted they cried, 'We must go to the Equator to die. The national honour requires it.'

Hardships began immediately, and on the first day they were persuaded that Antinori ought not to accompany them. The inhabitants were treacherous and ferocious; lions and leopards sprang out from the tall grass, and serpents coiled near their tents. The sun scorched, insects annoyed them, and the rivers were broad and deep. They were obliged to burn part of their stores; the guides refused to lead them; they swam rivers filled with crocodiles, and transported their boxes on rafts guided by a rope across the streams. Scarcely had they left the dominions of Menilek when the native chiefs refused to let them advance, considering them spies of that formidable enemy.

Menilek, his cousin Prince Masciascia, and every chief along the way, advised them to desist from this perilous undertaking, in which both man and Nature opposed their progress. There was war between Shoa and Galla; the Shoan general, Uorcò, with 5000 soldiers, accompanying them to the borders of the Galla country. The drums at the head of the army beat slow or fast according to the marching of the men. Some celebrated the deeds of their generals in song, others laughed long and loud at the jokes of the buffoons. The variety of tints in the faces of the men, their strange head-dresses, their white mantles listed with red and flying in the wind, the rich gear of the horses, the shields decorated with gilt filigree work, the shining of the lances, of the swords, and of the bracelets, offered a fantastic and picturesque scene. Right and left on the road were the houses left by the frightened Galla, who were seen in the distance spying every movement of Uorcò. He planted his tent on a hill, before the battle, to treat with the Galla chiefs for the advance of Cecchi and Chiarini, but his people became lawless, and the battle took place before the treaty was made.

Their departure after the Shoans were victorious excited the wonder of the army, and the soldiers all sought to dissuade them from advancing. But contrary to their fears the first Galla chief, Odolliè Batassiè, received them kindly. He was a fine type of the Galla race, tall, and proud-looking. His arms were entirely covered with brass rings, each of which represented an enemy whom he had killed. Although he had lost part of his wealth in the war, the chief gave them an ox to eat in his honour, and invited them to his own hut in the evening, where they were presented to his family. He considered them brave, strong men, and asked what 'medicine' or safeguard they possessed that they were able to pass safely in the midst of so many wicked people. If they would tell him the secret, he said he would be their friend for the rest of his life. They told him they had no 'medicine,' and that the only reason they could travel thus safely was the power of Italy, which protected them even in Africa.

The chief listened open-mouthed to this explanation, and at every phrase they uttered embraced them, taking good care, however, never to touch their feet, which being covered with shoes had for him a very equivocal appearance. His two daughters, really beautiful girls of seventeen and eighteen years, with black eyes, dressed in short skirts made of skins, examined the travellers thoroughly, and when their hands were pushed against the dreaded boots by a mischievous brother, ran away with startled cries. The friends of Odollie, who examined the guns with great curiosity, concluded that the devil was inside to make them go off. Before leaving this chief they presented him with a magnificent *sciammà*, or white silk mantle, which he received almost weeping with joy.

At the Huash river, which marked their entrance into the unexplored region, they were assisted in crossing by fifty nude Gallas, who splashed in and out of the water to show its depth, up to their waists, and led the loaded mules across. On the opposite shore fifteen or twenty chiefs, straight as bronze statues, in martial attitudes, awaited them. Their fierce aspect, the numerous bracelets on their right arms, and the long lances on which they leaned, inspired little confidence in the hearts of the explorers.

Abbà Garè, the next chief, was rough, unkind, avaricious, and proud, giving them nothing without an equivalent, and demanding, before letting them enter his house, a magic remedy to cure his son of insanity. To satisfy him, they were obliged to kill a crow, in which he believed resided the spirit of the person who had injured his son.

Glad to escape from this inhospitable black man, although suffering from fever taken on the miasmatic banks of the Huash, they mounted their mules and rode on over a country filled with gigantic sycamores, acacias, and mimosas, to the territory of Dullò Manissà, chief of Tuca, who annoyed and taxed them more even than Abbà Garè had done.

The people here were tall, straight, and well-proportioned, dignified in manners, and of a lighter colour than the Ethiopians. The thick crisp hair of the women is arranged in fine curls around the head and over the eyes, while the men have it cut in such a way as to give them a ferocious appearance.

At every village or hut along the way they were stopped by hundreds of Gallas, who appeared as if by magic, demanding gifts and trying to prevent their advance, because they were the friends of King Menilek whom they hated. The Gallas laughed when Cecchi and Chiarini reeled from the weakness of fever, and refused to give them even a drop of water. They would let the white men neither go forward nor backward, nor set up their tents. Five or six hundred individuals held long assemblies, hours in duration, while the sick men and their worn-out mules waited in misery. Even their servants threatened to leave them, and it was only by the eloquence of the guide and numerous presents to the Gallas, that they were enabled to proceed.

They had just started to leave Tuca, after sending other presents to the chief Dullò Manissà, when it began to rain as it only can rain in such a climate. The narrow road through which the caravan passed became a stream, the fields near were so many lakes, and they sank knee-deep in mud. Not a single Galla was on the road, and no human voice reached their ears. The only sound was the noise of the waters rushing down the mountain and breaking trees as it came. The cabins of the Gallas, isolated on the summits of the surrounding heights, seen through the rain, seemed the refuges of people escaped from a flood. When this ceased, and the sun came out, new troubles assailed them. A group of seven or eight horsemen, headed by three chiefs, galloped forward and ordered them to stop. This was the spot where Prince Masciascia, the cousin of Menilek, had once massacred many of the inhabitants, and these fierce avengers seemed disposed to make the Italian explorers pay for his evil deed. The guide Guddettà gave the savages the most beautiful objects remaining in the baggage, and on his knees conjured them to desist from vengeance. 'These are not Amharas, they are not the friends of King Menilek. They come from far, they are another race, as you see by their skin, as white as that of babies; by their leather feet; by their pantaloons, all of one piece; and by the shield which they wear on their heads.'

But these arguments of the good Guddettà were not strong enough to induce the Gallas to let the party go on. They tried to irritate the travellers by rushing forward, brandishing their lances, two, five, or seven together; throwing themselves back in the saddle, as if to strike; jostling with the shield and the horse, until Cecchi and Chiarini brought them to reason by a show of revolvers and a resolute defence.

ANTONIO CECCHI.

The Gallas adore all the great manifestations of Nature, like the mountains, the streams, the forests, and especially certain trees, such as the sycamores. They have sacred woods, upon the trees of which they hang votive offerings, consisting of rags, locks of hair, strips of leather, pieces of gourds, and other things, which give the trees a strange appearance. They have a dim notion of a Superior Being, and believe in a future life of pleasure or of pain. On certain days they pray to God and to many other spiritual powers, whom they adore over a glass of beer or hydromel, and sacrifice a domestic animal. They have also a number of priestesses, whose malediction they greatly fear. There are two religious sects in Galla, one of which recognises as its head Abbà Mudà (father of the nation). This wizard lives familiarly with several large serpents in a grotto, and is chief of a tribe of shepherds. He as well as his followers dress in skins, let the hair grow very long, and anoint it with butter, and instead of a lance carry a stick, upon the top of which is fixed the horn of an antelope.

The Gallas of this faith undertake at certain periods long journeys to visit Abbà Mudà, and give him presents of oxen and cows. Those only who have never killed any one, or robbed, or driven into slavery can take part in this pilgrimage. They are armed only with a stick, and to indicate their humility cut off their hair near the ears and dress like women. As a sign of peace they make a sheep go before them on entering the villages, and receive presents from the women of food and drink, but not lodging, as they are vowed to rest during their journey under the trees. They are met on their arrival by Abbà Mudà, who conducts them to his grotto, introduces only the chiefs, and permits them to adore and to feed a serpent which keeps guard there. In the grotto he keeps several young men as slaves, who lead a miserable life with him and the serpents. The visitors, after feeding and adoring the serpents, say prayers invoking benedictions on the Galla land, and are then consecrated, or receive the oil which makes them priests. The Gallas who have made this pilgrimage exaggerate the perils they have encountered, and the miracles of which they were witnesses. Lions, they say, kept them company on the way; rivers divided to give them passage; and near the grotto of Abbà Mudà oxen were killed by invisible hands.

One of these wizards was the means of giving Cecchi and Chiarini liberty when even the affectionate guide Guddettà, with tears, had left them to their fate. Surrounded by 400 of the tribe Soddò, and weak from want of food, which they had not touched for twenty hours, they were even themselves discouraged. But the chief Turi-Galatiè consulted the priest, who, after lifting his hands to heaven and making a strange prayer, ordered them to be set at liberty. He consulted also the entrails of a sheep, and the augury agreeing, they were free, but only after being despoiled of many articles.

While in this kingdom they had a singular experience on a market day, when thousands of the people were gathered on a plain with products for sale. Armed with their guns, and followed by four or five servants, Cecchi and Chiarini went to the market, their appearance causing a general cry of wonder and alarm. In a moment they were surrounded by a compact mass of people, whose lances held up high formed serried ranks of steel. Every act of theirs, and the sound of their voices in the strange Italian tongue excited the savage blacks, who followed them about through the market as they went with their guns levelled to make way.

Their last host, Turi-Galatiè, at first kind and friendly, now asked them for a gun, and would not be satisfied until they had promised to give him an order on Shoa for one. He conducted them to the next chief, Imam, making a regular consignment of their persons to his neighbour. 'They are going to Kaffa,' he said; 'see that they pass through the kingdom of Gimma, or if the king will not consent, send them by another road.' 'Very well, they are welcome,' said Imam. 'To-morrow I will send a courier to Gimma.' But notwithstanding these fair promises, when they arrived at his capital, after crossing a river, with the fever upon Cecchi, and being drenched by a heavy rain, he forbade their entrance, and left them to pitch their tents outside the town. He proved a robber, and wanted guns. He invited them one evening to his cabin, and with mellifluous words began: 'Listen! you, like me, are great personages. Menilek has recommended you to me, and I will do much for you. But you must do something also for me. I am not a man like the Gallas, to ask you for blue muslin, beads, mirrors, and such things. I do not ask much, I have many enemies, and one of your guns would be useful to me.'

He wanted to disarm them by getting possession of their guns and those of their servants, and was ill-pleased when they only gave him an order for one on their chief Antinori at Shoa. At the residence of this wicked Imam of Cabiena they visited the market on a rainy day, and found four or five hundred people crouching down close together, under umbrellas made of the large leaves of a tree. After going round the market several times, exciting general admiration and wonder, Chiarini innocently disturbed the peace by rubbing a match upon his pantaloons. Terror took possession of them all, as they believed the fire came by magic out of his skin. Calm was not restored until he made one of their servants light a whole box of matches in the same way.

Before Cecchi and Chiarini returned to the miserable hut which Imam had assigned them, they received, to their surprise, a demonstration of affection from all the people in the market. The kindness which they had shown to one of their Guraghè servants, in redeeming him from slavery in Shoa, was related by him to a friend of that tribe whom he met at the market. The story was rapidly passed from one to the other, and all the people surrounded the Italians, dancing and singing songs in their honour. Several days later the relatives of these redeemed slaves arrived from the Guraghè country, and entered with joy into their camp, accompanied by a great number of other people, who had come expressly to see these two strange beings capable of working such miracles. The meeting of these slaves with their parents, brothers, and friends was one of the most touching scenes ever witnessed. This friendship with the Guraghè, who are a people of Semitic origin, and possibly descendants of a Hebrew colony in Abyssinia, resulted in a visit to them made by Chiarini, leaving Cecchi in Cabiena to guard their possessions.

Imam continued to treat them unkindly, and made no effort to send them on to Gimma; their position became every day more difficult and perilous, and this temporary separation was necessary.

Chiarini met in the Guraghè country new adventures not less strange than those already encountered. All the Guraghè complained of the

CHIARINI.

cruelty of Imam Half-naked they crowded around Chiarini, when he stopped at their villages, asking from what country he came, what religion he professed, and humbly asking him to show some of the wonderful things he carried with him. The Negus or king, who bore the euphonious name of Uociccadelebet, ate salt with him, and gave him a brass ring in token of friendship. Another king, with his guards, came out to meet him, saluted gravely, asked to see some of his objects, and was greatly surprised in looking through the field-glass, and hearing the ticking of a watch.

When he looked through a coloured lens, which showed everything red, he said to Chiarini, 'You will burn up all the world. But spare my country. You are a priest, and I love you; you are a man of God, and can do good to these poor people whom Menilek has robbed.'

The guard of the king also took Chiarini for a priest and a saint, imagining that the costume of a general of the Italian army (brought as one of the presents to the chiefs along the way, but which he wore because he had no other clothes) was a sacerdotal dress. They prostrated themselves on the earth and kissed his feet, asking advice for their maladies and troubles, prophecies, and his intercession with God to preserve the country from every misfortune. 'Stay with us,' said the king, 'pray to God for us, we are poor, but for God's people we would give all we have.'

These poor people call themselves Christians, in opposition to Mussulmans, but have no idea of Christianity. The king is a robust, fine-looking man, with an aquiline nose, gentle eyes, and long, straight hair. Finding that Chiarini must return as soon as possible to his friend left alone in the power of Imam, he desisted from asking him to remain, but begged him to return another time. Chiarini's fame as a saint and a prophet preceded him on the way, and he was everywhere met by an admiring people. They came to know their future and the fate of their children, brothers and sisters in slavery in Abyssinia and Shoa, constraining Chiarini to let them prostrate themselves before him. The least suspicion that he was not what they took him for, would have cost his life; and all he could do was to give evasive answers, and say at last, 'I have no books here. Come to Cabiena if you want to know all.'

At one place he passed with the chief in the midst of 1000 people, all of whom admired him and kissed the footprints of his mule. At another, a group of natives dressed in skins came to meet them, but Chiarini could not talk with them, as he did not know their language. But from the crowd a woman named Kensi, a slave whom he had liberated in Shoa, came out and acted as interpreter. She was very glad to see him, kissed his feet, and offered him food and lodging. Farther on he met Biezut, another woman slave he had liberated, whom he kept for an interpreter, and who served him well when he reached the village of Queen Berorè.

Arrived at a fence of bamboo, within which were nine well-constructed cabins, Chiarini alighted from his mule and waited. He saw only a few dirty faces peering between the sticks, until a beautiful woman, with skin between red and brown, small aquiline nose, a little and smiling mouth, small hands and long. straight hair, came out to meet him. 'Hubie membum?' said the queen, examining him from head to foot; which the ex-slave Biezut interpreted, 'Will you enter?' He followed her among her people, who kissed the earth as she passed. 'If this savage queen,' says Chiarini, 'did not laugh at my appearance, it must have been from compassion. I was barefoot, because in crossing a torrent my shoes had become wet and heavy; I was muddy from head to foot, my pantaloons were drawn up to the knees; my hat was on one side, and I wore the old, faded and dirty uniform of a general.'

The queen led him into a garden, where, seated upon a leaf of *musa*, with a lady-in-waiting beside her and a large circle of people around, she looked at him attentively without uttering a word. Then she ordered a woman to wash his feet with hot water, and finally asked to see his wonderful things —the watch, the compass, the field-glass, the magnet and the whistle. She had the air and manner of a queen. She wore a skirt of ox-skin, and another skin over her shoulders like a mantle; a ring of brass upon her fore-finger; six brass rings on each arm, and two on each ankle. She gave Chiarini gentle and generous hospitality, and in a serious conversation, interpreted by Biczut, invited him to remain and go to the wars with her. 'I cannot,' said Chiarini, 'for I am not a man of war, but I will pray God to protect you and destroy your enemies.' In his character of prophet and priest this answer was so satisfactory to Beroré and her people that they sang a song in his honour, torturing his ears by the discord and the monotonous wail.

When Chiarini sat down to take notes of his journey the crowd drew around to see what he was doing, but he easily drove them back by shooting off his gun in the air. Five hundred persons fell backwards at the explosion, knocking each other down in their fright. When he arrived at another place the people wished to see him alight from his mule, knelt before him and then left, singing as they went. Having explored the country of the Guraghè, and arrived, always ascending, at the uplands 8000 feet above the level of the sea, which are the confines of the Arussi-Galla idolatrous tribes, Chiarini returned to Cecchi in Cabiena, visiting on the way his royal friend, who desired so much to see him again.

United again, the travellers were able at last to escape from the power of Imam, taking the way of Limmù, as the King of Gimma would not receive them, and the guides would not go by the way of Guraghè. Their sufferings increased as their journey continued, and they were left at last in a strange and hostile country, having passed from one robber chief to another—despoiled, deceived, and ill-treated by all. When they reached the end of their doleful pilgrimage, there was nothing left for the Ghenne-fà, the rapacious Queen of Ghèra in Galla.

Their mules were drowned or starved, their people were dead with fever or had deserted them, and every robber-chief along the way had chosen for himself the most valuable articles out of their boxes. Ghenne-fà saw that they had no guns, no rich carpets, no jewels or silks for her. She could not understand why they had undertaken so perilous and difficult a journey, or why they desired to pass through her kingdom. But they told her that their king wished to know all the wonders of the world, in order to write them down in his great book; and, as he had heard that beyond Kaffa there were mountains that threw out fire, and are always covered with snow, and little men, and the wild unicorn horse, he had sent them to travel through those countries.

But the queen, believing they knew the secrets of many arts, resolved to keep them as slaves, and exacted of Cecchi carpets, stuffs, and arms, and of Chiarini mirrors and ornaments. Chiarini succeeded in making a mirror that pleased her by using the glass of an old Arab lantern and the mercury from a scientific instrument. But at last, worn out with grief and disease, Chiarini died, leaving Cecchi desolate. This slavery was harder to bear than ever alone. He fled, but was retaken, and kept in a dirty hut, where he was watched night and day, and allowed only a little bread and water. Once he was condemned to be eaten by the crocodiles, but at the last moment was saved from this fate by the cupidity of his tyrant.

'Tell me your secrets, or I will have you drowned in the Gogeb.' 'But I have no secrets; I came here to learn. What *can* I make you? I cannot weave a carpet, but will paint flowers on linen cloth.' The queen was pleased with this, and gave him double rations of food.

But the hour of relief from this torture at last came, Antinori having persuaded the King of Abyssinia to reclaim the prisoner and threaten the queen with invasion. She then tried to make

Cecchi forget her ill-treatment and persuade him to call her 'his kind mother.'

The meeting of Cecchi, as he went in triumph, accompanied by an almost regal escort along the shore of the Blue Nile, with his liberator, Gustavus Bianchi, is dramatic. In the distance Cecchi sees a European mounted and a number of savages. He rises on his horse and calls out over the river, 'Who are you, generous man?' 'Bianchi.' And Cecchi, weeping with joy, answers, 'How are my family?' 'All well.' 'Is it true that Victor Emanuel is dead?' 'Yes, he is dead.'

The inundation of the Nile kept Cecchi waiting not less than four months upon its banks, but his sufferings were over. He received great honours on his return to Rome, and after a short repose returned to Africa.

His work, in three volumes, entitled *From Zeila to Caffa*, has been published at the expense of the Roman Geographical Society, and he is now Italian consul at Aden.

The region then traversed by Cecchi and Chiarini has since been conquered by Menilek, King of Shoa, and any of his friends could now travel there in safety. The petty chiefs, who were then suspicious and rapacious persecutors, would now receive with hospitality any travellers arriving from Shoa. They argue that when a traveller has been allowed to pass through the dominions of a neighbouring king he must certainly be either his friend or his messenger, and, conquered in battle soon after the liberation of Cecchi by a general of Menilek, they are now careful not to irritate him.

Menilek is strengthening and increasing his kingdom by dethroning the native chiefs, and establishing his own generals in their places. Gimma, Guma, Ghèra. Gomma. Limmù, Harar, and other places have fallen into his power, and he aspires to make the capital of this vast new kingdom to the south of Abyssinia in a city of Kaffa. The political and geographical importance of these conquests is evident.

The bones of Chiarini were wrested from the wicked Queen of Ghèra by another intrepid explorer, Augusto Franzoi, who brought them back to Italy and gave them to the city of Chieti, where Chiarini was born. He asked for himself as the only reward for such peril a lock of hair, which he divided with Cecchi.

Previous to this Franzoi had made several journeys in Africa, visiting Soudan, Abyssinia, and Shoa. None of the explorers have shown greater courage and ability in extricating themselves from difficult situations. While travelling alone in Abyssinia without a servant, and with small means, he was robbed by a chief of his mule and baggage, and forced to walk for days half-dressed, and with old shoes, to the capital of King John. Finding himself thus reduced to misery, he at first lost courage and went into a forest, where he wept for a long time, but recovered, and with incredible skill extricated himself at last from those difficulties and reached the hospitable land of Shoa. There Menilek received him kindly, 'because he was an Italian,' gave him presents, invited him to eat at his own table, and took him, together with an

Italian doctor living at Shoa, named Alfieri, to a war against the Gallas.

Tempted by curiosity, Franzoi willingly accompanied the king, but saw so much barbarity, sacking and burning of villages, carrying of youth into slavery, and murdering of women, children, old men, and the wounded, that his very soul sickened, although Menilek tried to mitigate these horrors. Two hundred and fifty thousand people followed the king to the war, but only about 100,000 were soldiers, and 15,000 of these had guns. The rest were women, children, and slaves.

In crossing a river he saw an immense number of these people, which he estimated at from five to fifteen thousand, drown, and for a time was separated from his friend Alfieri. Each sought the other in agony amid that wild and barbarous throng, and meeting at length fell into each other's arms weeping and rejoicing as if they 'had not met for forty years.'

With legitimate pride in his journeys, Franzoi, in the *Dark Continent*, published on his return, says, ' Let those who journey in less dangerous parts of Africa, well provided for by Governments and Societies, or using their own wealth, try to pass where I went, walking as much as I did, always alone, without arms ; poor, sometimes even without a servant ; often without food ; always without protection, or guide, or compass ; and they will understand that if I have not accomplished more it is not my fault.'

CHAPTER VIII.

DR. TRAVERSI.

DR. TRAVERSI accompanied the King of Shoa in one of his wars with Galla, where Cecchi and Chiarini suffered such hardships a few years before. This mountainous country has a high plain, like that through which runs the River Huash, about twenty miles square, where not a stone could be found, and where the fertile, alluvial ground is ten or twelve feet deep.

The people of Galla, to save the lives of their flocks during the rainy season, when the plain is inundated, have ingeniously constructed numerous mounds of earth near to each other, where their sheep and cows can find safety from the water and the mud brought down from the mountains, and also abundant pasturage.

The explorers followed Menilek and his victorious army over fertile plains and woody banks of rivers into the mountainous country of the enemy. In four days of fatiguing march they went around the mysterious Lake Zuai, which rests in the crater of an extinct volcano. The aspect of this lake is melancholy, high grass and wild tropical plants growing along the water and hiding it from view. It is a great mass of water, generally in motion with waves three feet high, and covered near the shore with a thick network of woody aquatic plants. Our explorers one day, in trying to walk over these, went down to the neck, dressed in white as they were, in the mud. There elephants roam at their ease, and hippopotami inhabit the muddy shores. The only path around the lake through the grass and shrubs was made for the army and travellers by the elephants that fled before them, and their feet slipped in the ashy, volcanic ground. The king was first in the woods after the prey, and first with his lance in battle.

Near Lake Zuai are two large volcanic rocks near each other, to which the natives attach a curious superstition. They believe that only the good—those who are beloved of God—can pass between them, while those who cannot are beloved of the devil. Thin men pass without difficulty, but those who are more fleshy twist and strain to procure this patent of sanctity, often without success. Once a year the blind, the deaf, the lame, and all afflicted with any disease, together with the curious and fanatics, meet at the lake by night to drink the water, which it is believed will effect miraculous cures. The Lake Zuai has five islands, one of which is inhabited by fugitives from a massacre that anciently took place in the surrounding country. It is said that they carried with them, and still possess, precious manuscripts relating to the history and religion of this district, and some believe they are Jews.

King Menilek twice endeavoured to take possession of this island, called Tullu-guddù, but, owing to the lack of boats for his army, was unsuccessful. But as the inhabitants, owing to the aridity of the volcanic soil, raise nothing for their subsistence, and make their purchases at two towns on the lake shore, the wily king will yet take possession of those towns and reduce the island by starvation.

The Gallas who live on the shore make light and elegant little boats from the wood of an aquatic plant that grows there.

The army of the Shoan king and our explorers then ascended to the high mountains by narrow, precipitous roads—horses neighing, men swearing, some under foot trampled into nothingness, and the others only reaching the end by feats of climbing and leaping that recalled to the Italian his early days on Mount Amiata.

They mounted to the high plain of Albassò, where the inhabitants subsist on meat, honey, and milk, and saw the springs of the River Uabi. The Guraghè, a tranquil, industrious people, conquered by Menilek, have long been so esteemed as slaves that their number has been decimated.

The slave catchers steal the women and children when they go to the springs or rivers for water, or dig long, subterranean galleries that open into the huts, and at night enter, kill the husband, and carry away the wife and children.

During this war, Dr. Traversi saw the parting between a woman and her two little boys, who had just been captured by soldiers of Menilek. The eldest boy wept and prayed to remain with his mother, and, when he could no longer cling to her, stretched out his arms towards her while they carried him away. In general, these poor people, once made slaves, accept the position quietly, only showing. by a fixed expression upon their faces, scorn for their captors. Menilek, persuaded by Count Antonelli, frowns upon slave-stealing, and is not responsible for all that is done by his soldiers.

The Guraghè women braid straw mats with which to cover the roofs and the floors of their huts, cultivate little gardens, make straw baskets almost as pretty as those of Florence, and are clean and gentle in manner.

The women of an adjoining tribe, on the contrary, are careless and dirty, talkative and gay. Dr. Ragazzi met a number of these returning from market, who made him endless compliments—asking after his health and that of his relatives, friends, and flocks—all with a gay and frank air; and one, with a smile, said, 'Don't stop at our house. We are poor—poor. and have nothing to give you.'

Tribes near each other are as different in language, dress, manners, and customs as their lands, the high. endless mountain plains, contrast with the low, volcanic lake regions.

Fatima, the wife of a chief of one of these tribes, presented Dr. Ragazzi with coffee, butter, and cakes, and waited patiently for his gifts in return. She was delighted with the earrings, beads, handkerchiefs, and mirror that he gave her, but yet asked for other things, saying, 'Not for myself, but for you; for if I can say that you gave me much, your name will be great, and I can then present you to all my relatives;' and she was as good as her word.

The pewter cups, the coffee machine, the carpet of the Italian explorer were all objects of wonder to this African Mussulman queen, but most of all his watch. She cried out, when she saw it and heard its ticking, 'Ohè, Arabbè! Ohè, Arabbè! Who is inside of your watch?' All travellers, to them, are Arabs.

These Ethiopian mountains are chiefly volcanic, and lakes in the deep, funnel-shaped, extinct craters are frequent. The tranquil waters of Lake Arra Scietan are so far down the steep sides of the rocky walls that the head swims in looking over, and the negroes say, 'If we look too long the waters will call us.' The fancy of the inhabitants peoples this lake with spirits, and attributes miraculous virtues to its waters. They say the lake is full of gold; that at night a red-red flame walks upon the water, and the cocks which live down there crow as the flame goes forward.

Another excursion made by the Italian explorers was to Rogghiè, five and a half hours from Entotto, which is a centre of the trade in 'black ivory' for that region. The day before their arrival 1100 slaves passed through the town, only one of whom —a boy—succeeded in escaping. The traders are Mussulmans, all of whom are irritated against Menilek on account of his prohibition of the slave-trade in his new dominions. Rogghiè is reached from Entotto by a zigzag mountain road, and the town itself lies at the foot of Mount Jerer, the ascent of which is fatiguing. The mountain is destitute of trees, but covered with high grass. There are few birds, but swarms of grasshoppers and many deer. Once on the summit a splendid enchanting panorama is spread out before the eye; an immense plain, slightly undulated, covered with crops of grain—some dry, some just out of the ground, and others ready to be harvested—stretching to the foot of a long straight chain of small spent volcanoes, strange in shape and treeless, and the crater of every one reflecting the sun, like a mirror, from the quiet waters of a lake. Wherever the Italian doctors went they were surrounded by throngs of the sick; their potions were swallowed with blind faith, and every prophecy of renewed health or certain death was received unhesitatingly. The crowds in the market-places separated before them as if by magic, and they passed through two lines of people, who reviewed them from head to foot—their hats, their shoes, their coats, and everything they wore were thoroughly examined. The old women looked sideways out of their cat-like eyes, and children cried desperately at sight of them, or, if they could, ran away.

Farther on in this mountainous region is the country of the Arussi Galla, where the power of Menilek is not yet established. His uncle, Ras Darghiè, whom he had appointed governor of that vast, unconquered province, entrenched himself in a strong natural fortress upon a mountain surrounded by deep, inaccessible precipices. His communications with Menilek were cut off by the rainy season,

and he was in danger of surrendering to the fierce
Gallas. But he went out and almost destroyed
them in a bloody battle, obliging the remnant to
abandon the country. Menilek then relieved the
army, which was suffering from famine, and, crossing
the other districts of Galla, took Harar, a large and
fortified city, in January, 1887. Harar, the ancient
metropolis of all the fertile Galla country, is 5400
feet above the level of the Gulf of Aden.

This important conquest of Menilek, friendly to
the Italians, is an improvement on the government
of the emir whom he has overthrown. This emir
was responsible for at least one of the three mas-
sacres of Italians which have taken place in Afar
and near Harar in the last few years. The other
two are attributed to the cruelty of Mohammed
Anfari, of Aussa, a chief of the Danàkili.

The exploring and commercial expeditions of
Giulietti, of Bianchi, and of Porrò were massacred
in that terrible desert which lies along the Red Sea
and the Gulf of Aden, and which must be crossed
by the caravans that would reach the fertile mountain lands of Abyssinia, the Shoa, or Harar. The
two Italian possessions on the Red Sea—Massowah
and Assab—are at the extremities of this region.
It is a frightful, sandy desert, undulated by low,
spent volcanoes, and looks as if it had been passed
over by a gigantic conflagration.

The horrors of Sodom and Gomorrah after their
destruction may be supposed scarcely less than those
of Afar, inhabited by the savage race of the Danàkili.
The valleys, burned dry during the summer, are rank
with decaying vegetation after the rains.

The palm, the acacia, and high grasses alone grow here; and the River Huash and its tributary, that come down from the mountains, instead of pouring into the sea, become wide pestilential marshes in the sandy soil. There is no agriculture. The cattle of the Danàkili browse upon the scarce vegetation growing among the rocks, and are watered from wells dug here and there. The climate is tropical, tempered only by the monsoon, and varied by frightful tempests accompanied by storms of sand. This is Afar, inhabited by 150 tribes of Danàkili, who love their land, such as it is, pine away or die if absent long from it, and hate the people of other countries.

They need the tropical heat of their climate, and shrivel up in the cold like serpents in winter. Picture these fierce children of the desert, tall and dignified like the Arab; of chocolate colour; little more than skin and bone, from their diet of sour milk; the legs slightly curved outward; the hair, black as a raven's wing, combed up in a bunch on the top of the head, curled on the sides, bathed in rancid grease, and shaved off like a wig behind; the face, arms, and legs tattooed; the nose and lips thin and regular, and the eyes bright and black. They generally go barefooted, but carry sandals to put on in rocky places. They wear around the waist a red-and-white striped apron, and over that a rectangular white wrap reaching to the knees. Necklaces and bracelets of beads or pieces of brass, and numerous little leather bags tied around or on the arms, containing verses of the Koran, as preservatives against the evil eye, disease, or danger, complete the picture—except, indeed, the lance, which is their constant companion. The women wear the outer white garment longer than the men, and reaching to the ankles; a blue cloth over the breast, and another on the head. Long, crisp curls cover their heads; the ears are bored in two places for heavy rings; and their ankles are encircled by rings so heavy that they walk like chained prisoners, and often cannot walk at all because the skin is broken. The women also are tattooed, and wear the charms which are supposed by every Mussulman to be a protection against evil. They are shepherdesses, and when they are out with the flocks, braid straw mats from palm-leaves, instead of knitting or spinning, as in Europe.

This is the sole art of the country, the mats serving to cover their tents and the huts of the camels—for beds, for carpets, and for salt-bags. The women do all the work at home and out of doors, while the men when at home live in absolute idleness, gossiping, and chewing tobacco. The tic-tac of the cream in bags of skin, which they beat patiently up and down to make butter, is heard by the traveller betimes in the morning.

Although ferocious and inhospitable to strangers, the Danàkili are extremely courteous and affectionate to each other. The young kiss the hands of the old; they ask a thousand questions about the health of each member of the family, about the house, the flocks, and the fields. In their councils of war, when all are seated on the ground, with legs drawn up, and the lance erect between them, no one is interrupted when speaking, and all are treated with respect.

The sovereign of one half of these tribes, without whose consent nothing is done in the land, is Mohammed Anfari of Aussa. He is fierce, cruel, superstitious, and afraid of white men, but covetous of the advantages which their commerce may bring him. His capital is Aussa, and there he received Dr. Traversi under the shade of an acacia, seated upon a stone, and surrounded by thirty of his warriors, all with the lance between their legs.

His neck, breast, and arms are covered with amulets to protect him from the white man's eye, as it was once foretold him that the first time he looked a European full in the face he would die. On this account he was hostile to the expeditions which crossed the desert going to Shoa, Abyssinia, and Harar, but was finally persuaded by Antonelli that the peril might be averted by charms, and his purse filled without danger. Unlike the other Danákili, he is fat and large, with a round face, full beard, and short, curly, iron-grey hair, with deep wrinkles furrowing his wide forehead. He has sixteen or eighteen wives, and all the children about the place are his.

GUSTAVUS BIANCHI.

CHAPTER IX.

RECENT ITALIAN EXPEDITIONS IN NORTH-EASTERN AFRICA.

IN Afar three Italian expeditions have been massacred, with the consent of Mohammed Anfari and the Emir of Harar. The first was that of Captain Giulietti and Lieutenant Biglieri, who, with thirteen Italian sailors from a war ship anchored in the Bay of Assab, left that place in 1882 to explore the country and find roads leading towards Abyssinia.

Assab, which has cost the Italian Government great expense, is useless unless roads are opened to the interior, by which the riches of Africa can find their way to Italy.

The brave young Lombard Giulietti with his

party were massacred in the night while sleeping, by the Danàkili, at a short distance from Assab. A rough granite monument now marks the spot.

Not long after this, in 1883, an expedition, of which Gustavus Bianchi was a member, visited the Negus of Abyssinia to carry him presents from King Humbert, and arrange a treaty of commerce. Bianchi, having completed this mission, continued

CAPTAIN GIULIETTI.

his journey with three companions, Salimbeni, Diana, and Monari, to the highlands of Ethiopia, bearing gifts to the King of Goggiam, who had aided in the liberation of Cecchi. There, on his return, he left Salimbeni, the King of Goggiam insisting on having a bridge built over one of his rivers, and caring nothing for the pretty baubles sent by King Humbert. Bianchi, with Diana and Monari, returned to the capital of Abyssinia, and prepared to cross the desert in the direction of Assab, to search for the bones of Giulietti.

This was against the warnings of the King of Abyssinia, who assured them that, although anxious to protect them, he could not do so, as they would be in danger from the Danàkili, and that water on that route was scarce. After wandering about for eight days, lost in the sands and finding no wells, deserted by their servants, guides, and interpreters, they returned to the confines of Abyssinia. When they again started out, they left behind nearly all their baggage, but determined to reach Assab by the route they had chosen. The Danàkili, from the tops of the hills near, held long conversations in the night with a treacherous servant, whom Bianchi had bound with ropes, and the next day the number of their attendants was reduced by desertion to six.

But Bianchi, urged by the desire to find the bones of Giulietti in this unexplored region, pressed forward, and even, persuaded of the good faith of seven Danàkili who presented themselves to him as friends, admitted them under his tent, and ate and drank with them. 'If you are really friends, show me,' he said, 'where are the bones of Giulietti.' On the very night of the massacre the savages led him to the spot at the foot of a mountain, and near a small lake. Towards evening they ascended the mountain, from which they could see Assab in the distance. 'There is Assab; we are near,' they said; but they never reached it, for they were surprised in their sleep, pinioned, and murdered before Bianchi could do more than give one cry for his faithful servant.

These savages will not bury a white man or touch his bones, for fear of contamination, and thus it was possible several years afterwards to gather the piteous relics together that had been exposed to the wild beasts, whitened in the sun, and almost covered with sand, and bring them back to Italy.

In April, 1886, another party, consisting of Count

CARLO COCASTELLI DI MONTIGLIO.

Porrò, President of the African Commercial Society of Milan; Count Cocastelli of Mantua, a Secretary of the Geographical Society of Rome; Professor Licati of Naples, and others, were massacred while on their way from the sea-port of Zeila across Afar towards the south to Harar. The object of Porrò was to open a commercial route with Harar; Cocastelli and Licati being added to pursue scientific studies along the way. A band of Mussulmans sent by the fanatical Emir of Harar met the

Italian expedition near Gialdessa, a native town under the English protectorate, of which they first killed all the garrison. They bound thirteen of the escort and took possession of all baggage, but left the Italians their horses and arms, assuring them that their lives were safe. But as they advanced towards Gialdessa and Harar they held a short discussion among themselves, and then fired upon the Italians, killing them immediately. At Gialdessa the native escort were freed from the ropes that bound them and permitted to return; but, overcome by terror and fatigue, only four reached Zeila, and of these four, only one crossed the Gulf of Aden to carry the dreadful tidings.

The expedition had crossed the level desert plain covered with low bushes, and was approaching the highlands of Harar. The roads were narrow, through rocky walls, on the summits of which they occasionally saw the natives seated as usual with their lances between their legs, and looking grimly down upon them. Flocks of white sheep browsed on the hill-sides and the chase was abundant.

Count Cocastelli, wearing a coffee-coloured suit, dark spectacles, and a broad-brimmed straw hat, made collections of butterflies, minerals, and plants. The letters of Porrò, Cocastelli, and Licati, received after the news of their death, were full of hope and interest in their work. But their imprudent confidence in their own courage and peaceful intentions led them to disregard the warnings of the friendly natives, and cost the lives of these explorers, as it had done those of Bianchi and Giulietti.

The bones of these brave men also lay where they fell for months, until they were gathered and transported to Milan, where they were buried with honour.

These repeated outrages induced the Italian Government, soon after the murder of Bianchi, to take possession of Massowah, an island on the Red Sea coast, which, without belonging to Abyssinia, was useful to her as a port for her products.

Through the influence of England, Italy was able to take quiet possession of the island, which was at that time occupied by the Egyptians. England was then engaged in the Soudan War. After Khartoum fell, the Italians remained at Massowah, with the temporary consent of the European Powers, though against the wishes of Abyssinia, and thus—though dangerous complications have since arisen—became masters of the eastern Red Sea coast from Massowah to Assab.

The city of Massowah, with 6000 inhabitants, is situated upon the island of the same name, which is one of several coral islands, so near the shore that one of them is connected with it by the accumulation of sand.

The climate of the island is tropical, but it is destitute of vegetation, except a few resinous plants. Its chief importance is due to its fine harbour, deep enough for the largest ships that pass the Strait of Bab-el-Mandeb. Remains of ruined cisterns made in the Persian style prove the antiquity of this town.

There are now, in the most prominent positions, a few modern buildings, and farther on is the

Arab city, with its mosque and bazaar glowing in Eastern picturesqueness of colour beneath a burning tropical sun.

Those of the inhabitants who can do so go to the mountains of Bogus in summer to escape the heat, or, without going so far, build on some low hills, about two miles distant, small huts made of boughs laid over poles stuck in the ground, with skins over all. Dry leaves laid on the ground inside, with skins thrown over them, serve as beds or sofas for the family, and an outer fence, built like the hut, serves to hide the women from view. There is no grass in the dry season, but the deep wells furnish water in more or less abundance.

Caravans descend from the mountains of Abyssinia in June or July, bringing in goat skins on the backs of mules, coffee, ivory, wax, gold dust, and spices.

Here the Italian troops, under General Genè, established themselves, taking possession also of Moncullu, or the 'Mother of All,' and Saati, towns twenty-five or thirty miles distant on the mainland. Saati, the most advanced of these stations, was one day out of food and ammunition, and in danger of being taken by the Abyssinians, who, commanded by Ras Alula, were in the vicinity.

Early in the morning 500 soldiers, under Colonel de Cristoforis, marched out from Moncullu with the provisions, anticipating nothing more than a little excursion from one town to the other. They went gaily over the slightly hilly country, and, at a place called Dogali, met a multitude of Abyssinians—some said 10,000, others 20,000. They were surrounded on the low hill, where they drew up to sell their lives as dearly as possible, and, when they had expended all their ammunition, were murdered with lances. When, at last, only the colonel and twelve soldiers were alive, they saluted, with their guns, their dead and dying companions, and a few moments after fell themselves. They were found a few hours later, by the company which left Moncullu in search of them, stretched out in line as if on parade—all dead or wounded. Only one reached Moncullu several days after, covered with wounds and in a pitiable condition. The wounded of Dogali were carried away in the arms of their companions, who expected to be attacked by the Abyssinians at any moment, and the dead lay there a prey to vultures and hyenas. The garrison of Saati made their escape in safety to Moncullu.

During the battle of Dogali, Count Salimbeni, who had been left by Bianchi three years and a half before with the King of Goggiam to build a bridge, was, with Ras Alula, on a hill near, a prisoner, and in chains. He saw the Italian soldiers advance with their bayonets glinting in the sun and the banner waving; he saw their brave defence against a horde of negroes, 'like a cloud that no man could number'; saw the remnant pierced with lances and stretched on the ground beside their fellows; and was then carried back by his captors to Abyssinia.

The story of Count Engineer Salimbeni is one of the most dramatic in the series of Italian explorations in Africa. His cruel imprisonment, together with Count Savoiroux, and with Major Piano and his little son Emanuel, eleven years old, by the Abyssinians, centred public attention upon them for months, and joy was universal when all were finally restored to their relatives.

The building of the bridge was the sequel to the liberation of Captain Cecchi from his imprisonment in Ghèra-Galla.

The King of Goggiam, persuaded by Bianchi,

COUNT SALIMBENI.

used his influence with the gentle Queen of Ghèra in favour of Cecchi, and for reward demanded neither jewels, silks, nor guns, but a bridge. A bridge to cross the Temcia in the season of inundation to the rich Galla country was necessary for him, and King Humbert could give him no other acceptable gift. He would have that, and nothing else, and Bianchi and Cecchi, who had waited four months for the subsiding of the waters, calling to each other across the river, knew that a bridge was needed.

Bianchi promised to bring a person who could make a bridge, but he knew well that the Italian Government, although willing to propitiate savages with gifts of chains, bracelets, brocades, and beads, would not build a bridge. All that he could do was to add the courageous and able engineer Salimbeni to his third expedition to Abyssinia and Goggiam. But Salimbeni was without money, instruments, or material, except what he could find in Goggiam, and had only one volunteer assistant, a bricklayer named Andreoni. Perseverance and courage must take the place of means, but his heart was not so stout that he could see his dear friends Bianchi, Diana, and Monari leave him almost alone in a strange land without sadness. He received their farewells and watched them depart, not dreaming that a few days would bring him the news of their cruel deaths. Then he turned to the task of making a bridge 150 feet long, 60 feet high in the centre, and with three arches, without bricks, without trowels, not knowing at first where to find sand or stone, or wood or ropes, with only one efficient helper, and in face of the doubts of the king and the scorn of the jealous people.

Their history said that the ancient Lusitani, before building the wonderful bridge over the Abai, slacked the lime with the blood of a thousand cows, and called down fire from heaven to dry the bed of the river; and when Salimbeni asked only for stones, sand, wood, and water, neither king nor people believed he could do what he had promised. 'He knows nothing,' they said; 'he has not asked for the blood of the thousand cows.' But the magnitude of his demands shook the eager desire of the king for a means of communication with the conquered land of Galla. He asked for men to make sixty thousand bricks, and instead were sent to him a few weak, half-starved women, each carrying her baby in a skin upon her back. Finding that King Taclè-Aimanot refused to furnish men and means, Salimbeni worked with his own hands until they were torn and bleeding. His appeal to the Negus of Abyssinia, of whom the King of Goggiam is a vassal, procured at last ample means and such help as the savages could lend.

He found stratified sandstone at ten hours' distance, of which he took 34,000 loads such as a man could carry, and sand and limestone in proportion.

The king and people were aghast, and said, 'These Europeans have come only to eat and drink. They ask for so much because they wish to do nothing. They cannot do what is a work only for God.' Even the Negus said, 'Let them try first a bridge over a little brook.'

But Salimbeni was not discouraged, although even food was scarce and bad, and he had very little money to buy it. Three old knife-blades, worn away before their duty was done, served to bore the rocks for the first planting the bridge; more trowels were made out of frying-pans, and hammers out of the native ploughs.

Finally the bridge is completed and the supports are taken away, the king aiding in the work. The great day of the inauguration arrives, and King

Taclè is to pass over it to pay his tribute to King John. The procession is formed. Salimbeni, on horseback, passes over, but finds that the king has turned pale and alighted from his horse.

Salimbeni returns to urge him to remount. When all have passed over safely, remembering the doubts, the insults, the thousand difficulties he has met and conquered, he calls out with a loud voice,

'Now tell me, O king, do you still believe that the Italians are liars and bad people?'

'No, no,' answers the king, with a tone of conviction.

'No, no,' repeat in chorus all who stand around. 'Great is the soul of King Humbert! The soul of Salimbeni is great!'

This demonstration was followed by a letter of thanks from 'King Taclè-Aimanot, true Christian son of Mark the Evangelist, tributary of John, king of the kings of Ethiopia—Greeting to Count Salimbeni, engineer. How have you passed these days? I, thanks to God, am well. I have seen the bridge, and it is much finer than the old one made by King Fasil over the Abai. I am well pleased, thanks to God. I liberated Captain Cecchi from Ghèra Galla, and have gained this in return. Now, if you will remain in my kingdom, look at my lands, and take what you like; I will give you servants, cows, oxen, sheep, and goats, and will accompany you to Galla, where I reign.'

After this success the king wanted another and larger bridge built over the Abai or Blue Nile, and, with excuses that his gifts for King Humbert were not ready, detained Salimbeni. But, finally persuaded by promises of return with other engineers, and perhaps an iron bridge, he took his lance, gold necklace, and other ornaments from his person one day at dinner, saying, 'Take these things to your king from me.'

Taclè-Aimanot has some idea of civilisation, and the character of his people would be good if they were not debased by a bad system of government.

MAJOR PIANO.

Some of them displayed generous and delicate sentiments, one bringing a fine elephant's tooth to Salimbeni as a present to defray the expenses of his return.

In Italy Salimbeni was received with honour by the Geographical Society, and provided with means for a new expedition.

In this he was accompanied by Count Savoiroux of Turin, Major Piano, and Emanuel Piano.

They had confidence in the natives, and went to Goggiam by way of Abyssinia to fulfil the promises already made.

But in the meantime the relations of the Italians at Massowah with the Abyssinians had become unfriendly, and the expedition had no sooner entered Abyssinia than they were made prisoners and subjected to cruel treatment. While trying to pass on to Goggiam they were invited one day, with smiles and courtesy, to the tent of the chief, and at a signal were seized by soldiers and chained. An iron bracelet on the right arm was attached to a chain half a yard long, the other end of which was around the left wrist of a soldier.

In this way they were sent on mules from one place to another, the guard walking, and their wrists swelling with the inevitable pulling. Salimbeni had an overcoat and thick shoes, but Savoiroux and Piano were exposed to cold, drizzling rain at night in thin clothing, and their light shoes were soon worn out. They were often called to the tent of Ras Alula to be questioned and threatened. A naked sword lay on a cushion before them, and the drums beat without, while Ras Alula cried ferociously, 'I will take off your heads! You, Salimbeni, are a liar; you came to spy out the land; and Piano is a great man—the brother of your general.' They all looked the savage calmly in the face, resolved to show him that Italians knew how to die with courage. Little Emanuel said to his father when the chief threatened them the second time, 'He is only trying to frighten us; he would have killed us yesterday if he meant to do it.'

In vain they protested that they were men of peace, and had returned to Africa to keep a promise, and to build bridges, houses, churches, and palaces. They were treated as spies with increasing severity, and became accustomed to threats of instant death.

COUNT TANCREDI SAVOIROUX.

Salimbeni and Savoiroux were carried chained to the battle of Dogali, and were exposed to the fire of the Italians. They were afterwards employed as surgeons, and threatened with death if they failed to cure the wounded. During the following month they were sent by turns to Massowah with letters from Ras Alula, giving their word of honour to come back, under penalty of the death of their companions, including the heroic child. Ras Alula hoped that the sight of their pale faces and torn clothes, swollen wrists and lacerated feet, would induce the Italians to retire from the positions they held. On their way to Massowah they crossed the desolate field of Dogali, saluting the bones of their countrymen, whitening in the sun, with the vultures flying above them. 'What matter,' said they, 'if we should die? So many of our countrymen have shown the courage of Italians.'

After four visits of the prisoners and their return to captivity, some concessions were made which procured their release. But Ras Alula pretended that one must remain; they might themselves choose which it should be.

Then arose a noble struggle between these 'dear brothers,' Salimbeni being very ill with rheumatism, which ended in Savoiroux's remaining four months longer alone, until he was exchanged for an Abyssinian bishop.

He became a tailor and saddle-maker, his feet being chained, but he kept his cheerfulness and courage through all. In a noble letter to his mother he writes: 'I am happy to have done my duty in liberating my dear friends from their chains, and I have done it with the greatest pleasure, knowing that you would prefer me dead and an honest man, to alive and dishonoured. True courage consists in meeting ill-fortune with resignation and religion. I think of you and of God.'

A few months later Italy sent 30,000 troops, the flower of her army, to avenge the massacre of Dogali, and made successful war with Abyssinia.

CARDINAL MASSAJA.

CHAPTER X.

CARDINAL MASSAJA.

ONE of the most remarkable characters of the modern Roman Catholic Church was the Capuchin monk, Cardinal Massaja, who died near Naples in August, 1888.

I have myself seen him of a summer day—a venerable man with a thick grey beard, dressed in the brown cloth gown of the Capuchin friars. He was seated in the garden of the Villa Ruffinella at Frascati, and surrounded by a number of the young priests residing in the college.

When near his eightieth year the order came to him from his superiors—and such commands neither age nor infirmity can resist—to write a history of his years spent in Africa.

The task was difficult, not only on account of his advanced years, but for want of notes, all his writings having been lost in the various exiles that he suffered from the seat of his mission. Yet Massaja has written from memory, and such other aids as he could procure in Rome, a work of seven volumes, which is illustrated by numerous engravings.

A large part of these reminiscences relates exclusively to his monastic character. Vigils, fasts, the celebration of masses, the recitation of the rosary, the improvising of chapels in upper rooms by covering wooden boxes with red cloth, and all the many forms and ceremonies of the ascetic life occupy much of the work. He gave slight attention to the natural sciences, except in the first years of his missionary life in Africa, when he had little communication with the natives from ignorance of their languages, and no time remained for these studies. He considered them extraneous to his mission, and time devoted to them as a betrayal of 'God, the Church, and souls.'

Monsignore Massaja, however, made use of a scant acquaintance with medicine and surgery which he had acquired when chaplain of a hospital at Turin. This, especially his skill in vaccination, procured him the good-will of the natives, and aided his missionary efforts.

Guglielmo Massaja was in the year 1845 teacher of theology in the Capuchin convent near Turin. At least ten years before he had expressed a desire to become a missionary in pagan lands, but, absorbed in his regular duties and verging on mature life, he had almost forgotten this aspiration of his youth, when he was one day informed by his superiors that he had been selected for a difficult mission to Africa.

At Rome, before sailing for Alexandria, he visited Gregory XVI, then on his death-bed. He was a great admirer of this Pontiff, of whom, on the contrary, the Liberal Italians retain most bitter memories.

For one reason or another all his movements were made in secret. He slipped away secretly from his scholars at Turin; he sailed from Europe in secret, and in secret travelled over Abyssinia to reach Galla. Dressed as an Arab merchant, under the name of Antonio Bartorelli, he passed through the diocese of Abba Salama, the native Bishop of Abyssinia.

In this journey through Abyssinia to Tigre, which lies beyond, the Roman Catholic bishop often traded or even slept with those who were in search of him; and Abuna Messias—the name given him by Abbà Salama—was unrecognised in the coarse dress and uncut beard of the wandering merchant. Once he was drawn up by a rope over a precipice to pass the night in safety in a hidden grotto. He crossed the rivers on square rafts, pushed forward at each corner by a negro in the water, or tied to a double rope, which a band of natives moved slowly around from hand to hand. Arrived at last within sight, from the top of a mountain, of the Galla land to which he was appointed missionary. Massaja declared he felt the joy of the Israelites when near the promised land. When, by crossing the last river, he actually stood upon it, he dropped the merchant's dress, arrayed himself in the brown Capuchin robe, and, with his companions, fell on his knees to chant a Te Deum.

He was not without adventures with wild beasts. One morning before daylight, as he walked alone in advance of his companions to recite his prayers, through a bamboo thicket on the crest of a hill he heard the soft step of a leopard as it trod over the fallen leaves. He wrapped himself from head to foot in a large piece of linen that he had with him, leaving only room to look out, while he clasped his crucifix the closer, and began to pray very earnestly to God. While his heart beat like a hammer, he saw the leopard turn when it came near, look fixedly towards him, and then pass on.

He once ran out of a burning prairie followed by a train of wild animals—leopards, antelopes, and serpents—that sought, like him and his companions and their faithful *asinello*, to escape. The donkey had his legs and tail burnt, and a large serpent, although it made prodigious leaps forward and upward over the burning reeds and plants, fell at last into that furnace, and was consumed. The natives are accustomed, in order to clear the prairies of serpents and animals, and also to prevent the vegetable matter from decaying after the rains and producing miasmas, to set the dry grass and shrubs on fire, keeping themselves out of its track. But that day the wind blew towards Massaja, who escaped from the fire with great difficulty.

He was nearly drowned in the night, at another time, by one of those terrific river floods that come sweeping down from above, and in a moment carry away man and beast and tree. He had chosen for the night's rest an island in the river, upon which was a large tree. This served as a refuge when the flood came. After eating his frugal supper, 'having still many prayers to recite,' he let his companions stretch themselves on the sandbank to sleep while he watched and prayed. His prayers ended, he stretched himself on the sandbank to sleep, but was soon awakened by thunder and lightning and the rush of waters, which compelled them all to mount the sycamore-tree. The island was soon covered, and the patient ass, tied to the tree, floated for hours with only his head above water.

At another time, when he had taken refuge under a fruit-tree during a storm, the fruit came beating down like stones upon him.

After his first journey to Abyssinia Massaja returned to Europe, visited France and England, made visits to Lord Palmerston in London, and to Mahommed Ali in Cairo on his return. And ascending the Blue Nile to Khartoum, he hoped to reach the Galla land from that side without passing through Abyssinia. But the mountains and the people both opposed him, and rendered it necessary to return by the Nile to a point where he could enter Abyssinia.

A visit he made on this journey to Galla, while

in disguise, to a shepherd people called Zellàn, in the mountains, is an idyl. He there reassumed his missionary character, and taught those simple-minded country people religion as he understood it; and they became so attached to him that they all wept when, after three weeks, he prepared to depart.

Massaja founded during his long sojourn in Africa numerous missionary stations in Galla, and also in Shoa, where he became the friend and adviser of King Menilek. His heroism was proved by the part he took in the war of 1879 between Menilek and King John of Abyssinia.

Menilek, then a tributary of King John, had taken advantage of the moment when the latter was engaged in war with the Egyptians to rebel, and persuaded several of the generals of the absent Negus to join him. Swift vengeance must be dealt out to the rebel, and the Negus, after returning victorious from the war with Egypt, turned his army towards Shoa, devastating the country and driving the miserable people before him to the capital of Menilek.

To the messengers sent to implore mercy, he answered, 'I am a Christian king, and must consider Menilek a heretic. as at the head of his clergy he has placed a Bishop of Rome, who has even converted to that religion Tecla-Sion, one of our best theologians. As the first condition of peace, he must send me both of these men. He must feed my army while it is in Shoa. He must pay me a tribute every year of 500 slaves, men and women ; of 50,000 dollars ; 500 mules ; 1000 horses; 50,000 oxen; and several thousand measures of grain, of honey, and of butter.'

Menilek preferred war to such hard terms of peace, and ordered all his people to prepare for the defence of their country. It was at this juncture that Cecchi and Chiarini, who were preparing for their tragic journey to Kaffa, found Menilek sad, preoccupied, and little disposed to aid them. Perhaps at another time, when the country was less agitated, and Menilek not so much occupied, their journey might have been more fortunate. The women and children and old people, with the cattle, retired to a place of safety; while groups of warriors armed with guns and lances were seen along the roads. Even the quiet valley of Let-Marefià echoed with the cries of war.

The rumour that Monsignore Massaja was the cause of this devastation by the Negus gained strength every day. As soon as Massaja heard this, he determined to go secretly to the camp of King John, and implore him to stop the war on Shoa, even if it must be at the sacrifice of his own life. But before setting out he wrote a letter to King John, which, unfortunately for his plan, fell into the hands of Menilek, and he was not allowed to depart, but was shut up as a prisoner in a fortress.

The Roman Catholic clergy of Liccè went out in procession to meet the Negus and ask for mercy, carrying with them some sacred stones, which they thought might have miraculous power to move him to pity. But the Negus became very angry, bound them with chains, and sent them back in that condition. The advance of the Abyssinian army alarmed the generals and the people of Shoa so much that Menilek was forced to ask for peace. He then swore fealty to the Negus, and as the first tribute sent him 1000 mules, 1000 horses, 10,000 oxen, and a number of slaves.

His dress on that occasion was a long shirt and pantaloons of silk brocade, the flowers woven in gold; a scarf at the waist of fine linen, the ends of which were embroidered with blue, yellow, and green silk, and a short sword ornamented with gold filigree work. The white sciammà covered all, and over that was the skin of a black leopard. His head was covered with a folded turban of fine silk, so that the butter with which his hair was dressed should not run down upon the bright silk shirt, and in the hair was a long gold pin, the token of royalty. Mounted on a richly caparisoned mule, Menilek, accompanied by 25,000 soldiers, went out sadly that morning to pay homage to the conqueror. His servant accompanied him, carrying in one hand the lance and in the other the shield covered with crimson velvet and decorated with gold filigree work, a horse's tail hanging from the centre. On his left stood an officer holding over him a large red silk umbrella to protect him from the sun.

But Menilek was sad and thoughtful, and looked like a victim ready for the sacrifice, while his dignitaries followed as if it were a funeral train. Having reached the imperial tent, within which sat John, with two enormous lions at his feet, tied only by a small rope to poles, and Persian carpets under him, Menilek descended from the mule, and tying up his sciammà in sign of homage, bent his forehead to the earth. The cannon of King John boomed twelve times as Menilek did this, announcing the fall of Shoan independence. The army of the Negus consisted of 70,000 infantry, 4000 cavalry, an immense number of slaves, and he had 6000 men and women servants.

The appearance of the camp was like that of a large city, where, instead of houses, were many-coloured tents of every size and form. When Menilek issued from the royal tent he found a mule with saddle and trappings ornamented with gold awaiting him, and 12,000 guns announced his departure. While all this was going on Monsignore Massaja was in the fortress where Menilek had shut him up in order to prevent his going to King John. He knew nothing of the peace concluded, or of the submission of Menilek, but saw himself pointed at as the cause of a terrible war. One night, with a servant and a young priest, he escaped down the steep side of the mountain, and presented himself in the tent of the Negus. 'You are ruining Shoa and its king on my account,' he said. 'Here am I in your hands.' 'What are you doing in Shoa?' said the Negus. 'I preach the religion of Christ.' 'But we,' answered King John, 'are already Christians. Go and preach your faith to the Gallas.'

G. P. WEITZECKER.

CHAPTER XI.

PASTOR G. P. WEITZECKER AND ITALIAN MISSIONARY ENTERPRISE.

ANOTHER missionary pastor. G. P. Weitzecker, a descendant of the Waldenses who kept the faith of old so pure in Italy, and whose bones lie scattered over 'the Alpine mountains cold,' laboured seven years in South Africa.

The Synod of the Waldensian Church, which meets annually at Torre Pellice, in the valleys of the Cottian Alps, was surprised in 1883 by the request of one of the pastors for a leave of absence of ten years. Pastor Weitzecker proposed to take the place in Basutoland, in South Africa, of the French missionary Coillard, who has since gone forward to the Zambesi river. The Synod, although reluctant to spare one of the few Waldensian pastors who evangelise Italy, consented, not a little proud at the same time of sending out its first missionary to pagan lands.

Early in the following year Weitzecker and his wife went to Africa as missionaries of the French society; first, however, making a tour through Italy to salute their friends and make collections in favour of their future work. The collections were small, as the congregations of Italy are poor, but the people listened with fervent interest to his accounts of the country to which he was going.

The long journey by sea safely accomplished, the two missionaries travelled overland in heavy carts to Leribe, the station in Basutoland. Along the way they were met by the Christians at the various missionary stations, who gave them a friendly welcome. One of these was Seta, the Christian chief of the village of Morija, who, with an escort of five or six men and change of horses, was going to visit his son, a student in the Scotch Missionary College at Caffraria.

Farther on their cart was surrounded by a company of twenty people on horseback, on foot, and in carriages, carrying three flags, and hurrahing at the top of their voices. These were white and black Christians, some missionaries and some converts, adults and children, who cried out, 'We are glad to see you, to greet you as brother and sister, and companions in our work.' 'And these were people,' said Mrs. Weitzecker, 'whom we did not know, and whose very names were strange to us,—people of other nations and of another race. Oh! the sweetness and reality of Christian brotherhood!'

In the carriage was seated the venerable wife of a missionary, who invited Mrs. Weitzecker to leave the cart and sit with her. It was touching when they met to hear this veteran of missionary life give her benediction to the novice. Followed by a band of twelve young negroes playing musical instruments, the travellers and their friends went to their first church service in Basutoland, where the sweet voices of the children in singing, and the sight of the Italian banner among others moved them to tears. This was their welcome to Basutoland, but the journey in the long heavy carts, drawn by from six to nine pairs of oxen under the broiling sun, against which the linen covers were little protection, continued.

After sticking fast at times in the streams, in the sand, and between rocks, so that the carts were more than once unloaded, they descried at last the mountains of Leribe and met Mr. Coillard. The next day they were presented to the tribe, and recognised by the chiefs as successors of Mr. Coillard This courageous missionary, ten days after, accompanied by his not less heroic consort, by a niece and by a young Swiss, left Leribe, the station which he had founded twenty-four years previously, and with a caravan of four waggons began the long journey to the Zambesi. There among the Barotsi he has founded a new work of peace and civilisation.

At Leribe the Waldensian pastor had 10,000

blacks to evangelise, scattered over a large territory. Thirty miles to the north, in a land of pure paganism, he founded another station, the chief, Gioel, being the rival brother of the chief of Leribe.

The church at Leribe, which seats five or six hundred persons, is often completely filled with a motley crowd, half Christian, half pagan. The bell, hung between two poles outside, rings twice, and then the congregation, followed by the minister, having deposited hats, turbans, canes, and clubs along the wall outside, enter all together. The men are on one side with uncovered heads, some dressed in European style, others with pantaloons and a blanket, or, if pagan, with only an ox-skin on the shoulders and a piece around the loins. The women on the other side of the church present a variety of coloured turbans and blankets, if Christian, and are bareheaded and almost nude, if pagan. The aisle is often filled with women sitting on the floor, who prefer this to the benches. The benches on the right are reserved for the chiefs and their families, and for the missionaries.

The province of Leribe is subject to constant wars, which disturb the missions, and the evangelist is often left without hearers because the people have fled. Prayer meetings to implore the special grace of God give excellent results. A young son of a pagan family who had fallen into vice, after being educated by the Christians, repented, called himself the chief of sinners, and cast himself wholly upon the atoning merit of Jesus Christ, the Redeemer, and by the indwelling of the Holy Spirit afterwards became a useful preacher. A woman, a real type of the savage, six feet high, with a ferocious countenance and half nude, wearing only an ox-skin around her, began to soften and asked to be prayed for. The chief, Selabolo, although yet a pagan, knelt at a meeting in the open air with others who declared their wish to be converted.

These results encouraged the Waldensian missionaries and repaid them for the hardships and trials they had endured. Sometimes the tears would come at the memory of their Church, their country, their relatives and friends so far away, but the thought that they were there by the will of God and the consent of their Church revived them. Mr. Weitzecker amused himself at intervals in collecting specimens of the musical and agricultural implements and of the weapons of war, ornaments, and clothes of the Basuto people, which he presented to the Ethnological Museum of Rome. This collection is highly prized by the Italian Government, which has conferred on him the title of Cavalier. He wrote frequently for the *Bulletin* of the Roman Geographical Society, of which he is a corresponding member, and was sent at the expense of the Society to visit the Italians living at the diamond mines at Kimberley. The first attempt to reach Kimberley was abandoned on account of the dry season, and they were obliged to return after having made a part of the journey. Several months later he set out again with his wife and one servant, travelling in a waggon, as usual. The journey this time was not without danger and difficulties of another sort. In November it was the want of food for the cattle, but in February it was the great rains, which had made the roads almost impassable, and the streams and rivers difficult to cross. But they passed from one farmhouse to another, courteously received everywhere, and losing only three days from the rain.

Although on a geographical excursion Mr. Weitzecker never forgot his missionary character, and relates how one negro youth wandered about four months in search of a school, and another wearied and worn presented himself at the school, saying, 'I am hungry and thirsty.' 'Very well,' was the answer of the teacher, 'we will give you something to eat and drink.' But he shook his head, saying, 'I am hungry for instruction—I am thirsty to learn.'

It is the custom in this part of Africa among the Boers, not only to give hospitality for the night to travellers, but to provide them with food for the journey. At one farmhouse, when the ostriches threatened to attack our travellers, the good woman of the house advised them to sit down on the ground, bury their heads in their arms, and let the ostrich flap its wings over them and shake them a little. 'It would not hurt them,' she said. Among the Boers they found people who although speaking only the Dutch language, bore the ancient Piedmontese name Malan, like Mrs. Weitzecker.

The city of diamonds and the region worthy of the stories of the Arabian thousand and one nights was reached at last, their waggon passing through the woods and garden-like fields, and over the red sand till their eyes were astonished by the electric lights and their ears by the busy hum of a modern city. In Kimberley and Beaconsfield, two sister cities, which in twelve years grew up over a tract of land three miles and a half in diameter, over four rich diamond mines, Mr. Weitzecker found 160 Italians. These waifs from Italy greeted him warmly, and were grateful for the interest shown in their fate by a society of the motherland. He exhorted them to be laborious, honest, economical, temperate, and friendly with each other, adding that if his mission had been religious he would have said, 'Live so as to honour the name of Christ,' but as it was merely civil he said, 'Live so as to render the name of Italy loved and honoured.'

The journey home to Leribe was not without emotions. Once they encountered another waggon, travelling in the dark at night, and both he and Mrs. Weitzecker were thrown out. At another time they were fast in the bed of a stream three hours, with rain threatening, and the flood from the upper stream expected at every moment. He took the most precious object, his wife, to the shore, and then by degrees all the goods in the waggon, which thus lightened was at length extricated by the oxen from the sand.

Other excursions, reports of which were sent to the Geographical Society of Rome, followed this. He visited the beautiful waterfall Maletsuniane, in the centre of Basutoland, which is 630 feet high, vertical, and so surrounded by precipitous rocks, like an immense well, that it is possible to ascend only in one part, and very difficult to descend. To look down from the top into that dark abyss, called by the natives 'Inferno,' it is necessary to lie flat on the ground and be held by the feet by two other persons. Even this protection is not enough to prevent dizziness and almost an insane desire to follow the mass of water that throws itself over that precipice.

In one of the journeys necessary for the care of the mission stations, he discovered a cavern, upon the walls of which were painted in red some curious pictures, made by the Boscimani. These represent cows, oxen, elephants, monkeys, and men and women. The largest picture has eighteen figures, and represents the flight of Boscimani women before some Caffir warriors. It is full of life, and not without artistic skill. The women are represented as pigmies and in a lighter red colour, while the warriors are giants with long legs.

But the health of Mr. Weitzecker gave way in 1889, and after a long illness he was forced to return to Italy before the ten years were ended.

The bridal journey of two other missionary Waldenses, Luigi and Maria Jalla, from the valleys of Piedmont to the Zambesi river was a long one. Sent out by the Society of French Missions to assist Mr. Coillard, they left Italy immediately after their marriage and were ten months in reaching their destination. They spent one month at Leribe, and then, as it was on their way to the Zambesi, accompanied Mr. and Mrs. Weitzecker in their excursion to Kimberley. Here they bought one of those enormous waggons drawn by sixteen horses used in that region, and hired two others for their journey to the equatorial region.

To these brave young hearts every strange thing around them was a pleasure. They enjoyed the cool temperature of April—the tropical winter time. The mimosa woods were filled with birds of many-coloured plumage, singing as sweetly as nightingales, and known to the natives by their song, some of which were as small as a little finger and others as large as blackbirds. Here too they saw the antelopes, grey on the back and white below, which always go in troops, with a sentinel at the side, who whistles at the slightest cause of alarm. At night they heard the howling of the wolves, and by day saw the damage done to roofs and furniture by the white ant. When the waggon was in motion they sat together in front talking or reading, and at night often sang the familiar and beloved hymns of home. 'This is the time,' they write, 'when thought flies most easily to our dear ones.'

They halted now and then at English or French missionary stations, where they were kindly welcomed. At Malopolele they found the chief Sechele, mentioned by Livingstone, living in a beautiful house upon a hill. Like all travellers in Africa, who sooner or later suffer thirst, they found no water as they went on, and could not eat. They dreamed of the waters of the Lake of Geneva and of drinking at a torrent, but at last found a stream into which the thirsty oxen plunged and drank before they could do so themselves. At another missionary station, among a population of 40,000, the church was densely crowded with hearers. The aisles were full of people seated on the floor, crowding the windows and standing in four rows outside, Khama, the good chief, taking his place with his family near the pulpit.

The first Sunday that Pastor Jalla and his wife spent by the broad waters and green banks of the Zambesi was for them a festival. 'I would not exchange this day,' he writes, 'for the treasures of the world. Our grateful hearts are bursting with joy. We have thought of it so long, and now it is no more a dream, but a reality. The goodness of God has abounded for us. He tried us on the way only to make us happier at the end of our long journey. Oh! how I wish I could fly like my thought, my dear ones, to give you this news, so that you might with us bless God.'

The station of Mr. Coillard was fifteen days farther up the river, but the old hero had taken that long journey to meet them. They had only to cross the river to be at home for the time with their eighty oxen, three horses, five negroes, and some sheep and goats, and were obliged to hire from the chief of an island in the river sixty-eight men, paying to each ten mètres of linen for the help.

When all at last were over, the beasts swimming and they in canoes, the friends planted their tents side by side and rested in the moonlight, talking of home and friends and their work until midnight.

Mr. Coillard left next day, and they were alone with four servants, their only guardians in that wilderness, except that 'One who never sleeps. The last night of their journey to their ultimate destination Shesheke was disturbed by the visit of a lion, which came within a few feet of their encampment, and was shot.

Thousands of leagues from their native land, their hearts thrilled with patriotic emotion as they read the *Cuore* of De Amicis in the evening, when all the men were asleep around the fire, and nothing was heard but the crickets in the grass, the frogs in the water near, or the growl of a hippopotamus. 'But do not pity us,' they say; 'we do not need it.'

The people of the Zambesi are accomplished beggars, and cannot say two words without asking for something. A crowd of black creatures surrounded them at every halt, and they took their meals in the presence of fifty or sixty, who watched every mouthful they swallowed.

They built a small wooden house at Shesheke with a stable for the horse and a chicken house, which the large serpents soon learned to frequent.

Pastor Jalla and his wife, as well as his brother, Adolfo Jalla, who had joined them, paid tribute to the African climate with fevers and other maladies.

The description of the return of the chief Morantsiane and his men from a war upon another tribe is picturesque. The day before, a messenger was sent to announce their arrival, and next morning several gunshots showed they were near.

Soon afterwards a long single file of blacks approached and formed a square, into which warriors with lances and shields entered jumping, and went out to the songs and cries of the others. Forty women formed a circle in the broiling sun, beating hard with their hands, singing by turns, screaming, and hitting their mouths with their hands as they made bows on all sides. In the middle of the circle several wives of the chiefs, the high aristocracy, danced alone for several hours.

Morantsiane wore a handkerchief on his head and a long shirt of many colours. Some of his men had nothing on but a tiger-skin or the skin of a monkey, a shirt, or a piece of stuff. Others had a long feather stuck in the hair or a wisp of herb around the head, a cap ornamented with shells, a crown of teeth or a rag tied in some ridiculous shape. Some blackened the forehead or the eyes, and others, to show that they had killed a man, had a white mark painted round the eyes. Morantsiane was delighted to see the missionaries again, and sat talking with them while some of his people built a hut for him to pass the first night in, after returning from battle, as he was not then permitted to sleep in a house, and while his wives came dancing in to greet him. This ceremony was curious. Each woman bent low to the ground before him, touching the earth first with the right side of her head and then with the left; then rising to sing and dance and at last kneeling and kissing his hands. The king sent the missionaries ten cows, part of the spoil taken from his neighbours the Mashikolumbos, but as they had disapproved of the war they felt obliged to return the gift with many thanks. This refusal excited great wonder, and some of the chiefs began at once to sing songs in their honour.

All the time they were away—three months—these savages did honour to the instruction of the missionaries by never travelling or fighting on

Sunday. They had with them two men of Zambesi who had spent two or three years at Morija in Lessuto, and could teach them on these Sunday halts.

One of the chiefs on his return said, 'Know, O Moruti (missionary), that I have not killed any man, and I ordered my son to let a woman go free whom he had captured.'

Signora Maria Jalla had visits continually from the women, fifteen or twenty of whom came at a time, and waited at her door for hours together. She tried to teach them, but as every day the scholars changed she made little progress. The people in a circuit of thirty miles, whom the pastor could visit on horseback, were glad to see him, and one named his first child Moruti or Missionary Jalla.

'More and more,' he says, 'I love this missionary life, and understand now why returned missionaries are often homesick for Africa.'

A woman came one day to Signora Jalla, saying, 'Mississi, do give me some medicine to cure my boy of stealing.'

They made many sincere friends among these savages, who were grieved when the time came to change their residence to Kazungula. They are now at a short distance from the Victoria Falls and the tribes of the Ma-Kololos, who still remember Livingstone with such love that some of them never pronounce his name without lowering their eyes in sign of the utmost respect.

May these Italian missionaries, like David Livingstone, honour Christianity in Africa, and be loved as that great man was!

COUNT PIETRO DI BRAZZA.

CHAPTER XII.

COUNT PIETRO DI BRAZZA.

Count Pietro Savorgnan di Brazza, although in the service of France, was born in Italy, which he left at thirteen years of age. He now calls himself a Frenchman, but his father, mother, and several brothers are Italians, and live in Rome.

While attached to the naval station established by the French Government on the deserted coast of the Gaboon, to prevent the slave-trade, Pietro Brazza in 1874 made an expedition up the river Ogowè. Before him Paul Du Chaillu had suggested that the numerous small rivers by which the Ogowè pours its waters into the Atlantic came from a large stream above, perhaps connected with the central lakes of Africa, and in 1862 had followed on foot one of the tributaries of the left bank.

Two officers of the French marine afterwards ascended beyond the delta, and proved the existence of this great river. It remained for Brazza, in several bold explorations through the lands of cannibals, often the only white man of his party, and without shoes, to ascend the river to its sources, and cross on foot over the few miles that separated them from the sources of another river (the Alima), which afterwards empties into the Congo. All this territory, a splendid acquisition, he has placed under the dominion of France. He proved that the Ogowè was not the same river as the Lualaba, about that time discovered near the lakes, the outlet of which was then unknown, but which was afterwards seen to be identical with the Congo.

Chiefly at his own expense, but with some aid from the French Government and scientific societies, Brazza, after a year of preparation, set out up the river, with ample supplies of salt, guns, beads, knives, and razors—objects which take the place of money with the savage tribes. He had with him three Europeans, thirteen black Mahommedans from Senegal, four interpreters from the Gaboon, and a cook, whose talent, however, served little, as Brazza carried with him only biscuits, rice, coffee, sugar, sardines, chocolate, and other prepared food.

He was conveyed by a French steamer to Point Fétiche, beyond the delta, and there kindly received by old Renoqué, the most powerful chief on the river, who was eager to have commercial relations with the mouth of the Ogowè.

Brazza there embarked with his company on four long boats adapted to passing the rapids. The banks of the Ogowè are peopled by various tribes, often at war with each other, who exact heavy tribute from white travellers.

The Osseyebas are cannibals, who fortunately, however, care little for the flesh of white men, but highly appreciate their merchandise. The Apingis acted as wreckers on the shore when several of the long boats were upset, and they robbed Brazza of a bale of tobacco and a large part of the heavy goods which he carried. The Okandas above the rapids received him kindly and let him establish head-quarters on their land, while he negotiated with the Osseyebas and the Adumas for permission to advance into their territory.

Brazza made acquaintance with Mamiaka, an Osseyeba chief, and leaving the Okandas, in company with only three men he went forward into this unknown country, inhabited by cannibals. But overcome by the fatigue and hardships of the way, and excited by the lies, duplicity, and cunning of the savages, his health gave way, and he returned in a boat to his head-quarters.

This second journey up the Ogowè was even more dangerous and fatiguing, but resulted in discovering the sources of the river. The courageous traveller was detained by the treacherous Adumas, who coveted the contents of his boxes. He only escaped from them by bribing with gold the grand Fetish man, or witch doctor, whose power over these superstitious savages is unlimited. He next went up as far as the Falls of Poubara, sixty feet high, where the river divides, and is no longer navigable owing to the frequent rapids and falls. On the banks of the stream he found the tribes of the Okota, the Sciache, the Auangi, the Sebé, the Obamba, and the Odimbo, the latter of whom use the short bow and barbed poisoned arrows.

It was clear at last from these explorations that the Ogowè was not a direct route to the centre of the African continent; and there was yet an immense tract of unknown country between its sources and the Upper Nile.

How was it possible for him to go forward in this maze of unknown rivers, mountains, forests, and savage tribes, constantly subject to the miasmatic fevers of the country, with heavy baggage, and with bearers who dreaded to leave the river, which was their road home, and often on the way threw down their loads, refusing to go farther? Up to this point Brazza had travelled through a fertile but unhealthy country, where provisions were abundant and the people friendly. But he had reached the bare rocky mountains and half desert land of the Batékès, a warlike tribe given to pillage, and almost destitute of food.

To replace the bearers he had brought from down the river, he employed slaves, giving them liberty from the first, which they used to desert him as soon as they reached their own tribes, thus rejoining their friends and relatives who had already sold them once as slaves, and would sell them again. To protect himself and his goods from the

Batékès, Brazza, when left with only three faithful men, early one morning buried a box of gunpowder, so that he could blow it up when necessary. This mysterious proceeding so alarmed the superstitious marauders that they called him a Fetish, and left him in peace. On this part of his journey famine was his constant companion, and he learned to eat, like the natives, white ants and grasshoppers cooked in palm-oil, which he soon found very good. Here he discovered the Alima, a river with several tributaries, and his route lay towards the centre of the African continent.

His progress through their land was opposed by the Apfourus, and he was attacked by the inhabitants of every village, often marching with his few companions through long lines of savages armed with clubs, when a moment of weakness would have been fatal. In the night he heard the beating of drums and sounds from the river shores and the tops of the hills like the neighing of horses, and saw watch-fires kindled all along the shores. He heard the enemy sing war-songs, the refrain of which was that his flesh would soon be eaten at their festival of victory. He took refuge in his boats on the river, and next day was attacked by thirty boat-loads of blacks, who were soon routed by the well-directed fire of his fifteen guns. But the following night Brazza escaped from this dangerous locality, and crossing, by the light of bamboo torches, a marshy forest, he reached at last some hills, and soon was out of the power of the Apfourus.

He returned to the country of the Batékès, which

he found desolated by famine, and even almost without water. He and his two white companions won the good-will of their followers by dividing food and water with them. The Batékès were won, but, sick and without means, Brazza resolved to leave this inhospitable and enigmatical land. Not until his return to Europe did he comprehend that the Alima was a tributary of the Congo, the great river of Livingstone and Stanley, and that he had crossed the hilly region of about fifty miles between the sources of the Ogowè and the waters of the Alima, there narrow but deep, clear, and navigable for large boats.

The swift and happy return down the Ogowè to the friendly Okandas, where he found new supplies, was almost saddened by a singular accident. The long boat in which was Dr. Ballay, the companion of Brazza in all these perils, was upset by a huge hippopotamus, throwing out the occupants and giving them a cold bath and a fright, but nothing worse.

At another time when a boat containing forty-four boxes full of the merchandise and the stores that were to serve for the journey slipped its moorings at night, and went down the stream, Brazza ran down the shore barefooted, cutting his feet on the rocks, and leaving his men at certain distances to watch the river. When he had outstripped them all, and walked for three hours, he prepared to spend the rest of the night on the rocks. He built a large fire to protect himself from the cold and the wind, and thought sadly of all the precious things lost; among them his instruments and documents. As day dawned, however, he saw his boat caught among the rocks at the foot of a large tree that grew in a narrow part of the river. He saved it from some thieving Apingis by firing a revolver over their heads, and then persuaded them to aid him in bringing it to land.

After three years of this adventurous life Brazza went to France; but soon wearying of an easy life, returned to the rivers and forests of Africa.

With the Osseyebas he crossed dense forests, where the sun was never visible, passing under green domes of leaves and branches, and wading over the brooks and streams when he did not cross them on the shaking trunks of huge trees.

In these long marshes, where even the men of the forest sometimes lost their way, he hung his hammock at evening, when the darkening of the forest showed that the sun had set. and the Osseyebas gathered sticks, leaves, and bark, with which they made huts, beds, and fires.

He gained the admiration and respect of the savages by killing elephants and wild bulls in the forest, which served them all for food, and awed them by his guns and revolvers, his fireworks and magnesium lights. The Adumas discovered by Brazza are a debased and brutish race. They are destitute of history or traditions, or poetic ideas, even the coarsest. They are cowardly and perverse, and sell their own children, fathers, and brothers into slavery. When they sing together in time while rowing. in order to row together, their songs have no sense or meaning whatever. They considered Brazza their prey; and, cunning and rapacious, despoiled him whenever they could, although professing to be friendly. They believed that he brought with him in his boxes the small-pox, which then afflicted the tribes along his route, and said, 'The white chief is wicked, and carries with him a box full of maladies. When he passes through a village he opens this box, and all the diseases fly out, which make our men die.'

But, by the care he took of the sick, and the medicines given by his companion Dr. Ballay, he persuaded them of his kind intentions. His rule when among these savages was always to be more severe on himself than on them, and to practise humanity and justice. His aim, he says, rather than to discover new lands or new tribes, was to carry civilisation to these unknown and distant countries. But he often failed in these humane efforts. At one time he found a savage whom he knew in slavery, and liberated him, but was surprised that instead of enjoying his liberty and continuing with him the savage returned to the same treacherous friend who had before ill-treated him and reduced him to slavery.

The second journey of Brazza, from 1879 to 1882, was made at the expense of the French Government, which he had persuaded of the value of this territory. He started for the Congo and the mouth of the river Alima, the upper part of which he had already discovered, at nearly the same time that Stanley travelled on the other shore of the Congo, at the expense chiefly of the King of the Belgians.

The contrast was great between the mountainous, precipitous country where Stanley travelled and the comparatively easy district traversed by Brazza to the north of the great African waterway.

At the confluence of the Ogowè with the River Passa, Brazza, in 1880, founded the first French station, and called it Franceville. It was in communication by the Ogowè with the Atlantic, and by an easy overland journey also with the Alima and the Congo.

An embassy came to him from Makoko, the chief of forty tribes. 'To the great white chief of Ogowè, whose terrible guns have never served to attack, and whose feet are accompanied by peace and abundance, Makoko sends the word of peace, and hopes to see his friend.'

Makoko understood the benefits of an alliance with the white man, and soon placed all his territory under the protection of the French flag. When the white chief expressed a wish thousands of black men were ready to obey it.

Makoko received Brazza one day in state. Stretched on a lion's skin spread over the red throne, his wives and children and courtiers, as well as the witch doctor, around him, he awaited the entrance of the explorer. The new ally, on his part, wore his naval costume, with gold buttons and bands, and was accompanied by his brother Giacomo, Attilio Pecile, and other Europeans. Thus, a friendly alliance was concluded with the chief whose power reached to the mouth of the Alima on the Congo.

The forty tributary chiefs of Makoko came—some from the Equator—to meet Brazza a few days later. It was a strange and imposing spectacle. He was their friend, not their conqueror, and they believed in the protection of the French flag, which was accepted and raised by every one of them. Yet more than once he was obliged to meet real battles with people of these tribes before he could persuade them of his superior force and skill. Brazza founded two stations, one on the Ogowè and one on the Congo, Franceville and Brazzaville, which are said to be self-sustaining. By these access is obtained to the Upper Congo, which leads to the heart of Africa. Navigation up the Ogowè to Franceville is easy, and the distance across the country to the point where the Alima is navigable is forty-five miles. The distance from Franceville to Brazzaville on the Congo is 180 miles. This is a fertile country and thickly settled. Brazza recounts that he once stopped with 700 men at a village near evening, and was not only fed, but he started next morning, by paying ninety pounds of salt, with provisions for two or three days.

After the second journey he was welcomed in France with enthusiasm, and received from the government large subsidies to make roads, improve the stations, and launch a small steam vessel on the Congo at Brazzaville. About 7000 natives in the basin of the Ogowè are at the service of France to carry weights and row on the rivers. Slavery and human sacrifices are diminished, and this population of 5,000,000 are losing their vices and cruelty by contact with civilised men. In ten years 450,000 dollars were expended by the explorer, and his judgment, patience, and endurance were beyond all praise. He is still there, although at one time recalled by the French Government. Italians naturally regret that a man of such energy should disown his country, and lay his life and achievements at the feet of another nation.

Count Giacomo di Brazza, a brother of the more famous Pietro di Brazza, was proud to call himself a Roman and an Italian. As a boy he admired the exploits of Pietro in Africa, and prepared to follow in his footsteps. He devoted himself to those scientific studies which had been neglected in Pietro's journeyings. He was a naturalist by nature and profession, and often, in the African wilds, when food was scarce, transferred a rare fish to alcohol for preservation rather than to the table.

The ardent desire of nine years of his boyhood was satisfied when he was appointed naturalist to the expedition in Equatorial Africa of Pietro di Brazza in 1883. He was to study the zoology, botany, geology, and ethnography of the country, and make collections to be sent back to France. Accepting this position without compensation, he only stipulated for the right to make another collection at the same time, and to add to the party his friend Attilio Pecile, son of a senator of Italy. The journey of three years and a half was made together, and their adventures were nearly the same, so that the account of one serves also for the other. Giacomo di Brazza says that he had learned to appreciate the learning, energy, courage, and abnegation of Pecile in various excursions made together in the Alps.

Giacomo di Brazza looked at Nature with a poet's eye, and saw beauty in the trunk of a dead tree, in the broad expanse of the river losing itself in mist, in a floating island formed of various trunks of trees covered with growing papyrus. He noted an elephant standing quietly in the midst of the aquatic plants on the shore, to let three large white birds search for parasites on his back, and the hippopotami sleeping on the sandbanks, the crocodiles yawning in the sun. Yet in all the splendour of Nature on the Ogowè, the Alima, and the Congo, the young traveller remembered with undefinable yearning his own distant Italy.

Boating was full of perils and excitement, as the long, light, narrow boats, hollowed out of the trunk of a resinous tree, were sent forward by the strong Adumas. Before starting, everything in the boat was bound tightly to it, so that in the frequent upsets nothing might be lost. Such boats are manned by seventeen Adumas, who row standing, and by long practice have become skilful in passing the cascades, the rough currents, and the whirlpools. Sometimes they draw the boat with ropes, wading over the rocks in the bottom of the river; sometimes they drag it along the rocky shore, or push it before them, and half the time these skilful boatmen are in the water. They start off on their journey singing, and row near the shore under arches of the fragrant tropical trees that lean over into the water and shade them. These mariners of the Ogowè transport 100 tons of merchandise each year in their frail barks, returning up the stream to their homes with merry songs. But often they do not reach their homes. The cold rain chills them at night after a day's hard rowing in the boat or pushing it over the rocks. They die of pneumonia or fever far from their own land, or are thrown out upon the rocks and killed.

The brother of the 'Great Commander' was received by the Okandas—a tall, handsome, and intelligent people—with friendly respect. 'We know you are his brother,' they said, 'because you have the same feet'—meaning his shoes and his white feet when bare—'and because you wear the same charm'—meaning a gold medallion worn around his neck, and containing locks of his mother's and his sister's hair. They thronged around him curiously—a wall of black human flesh—first the children, then the women, and behind the men. He did not delay with these, but pressed on up the river with his Adumas, through walls of giant trees bound together by trailing vines, until he reached a more open country, where green plains stretched away to the foot of low quartz hills. After three days' navigation Giacomo and Pecile found themselves in the land of the Pauens. These men are cannibals, but eat only their victims in war. They have a gun loaded with stone, and a knife. They wear many copper and ivory bracelets on the arms and legs; their bodies are greased from head to foot, and painted red; and they wear greased antelopes' skins. They have a hole pierced in the nose, into which they insert either an elephant's hair, to which beads are attached, a bit of wood, or a needle—not to lose it. Further on Brazza reached the country of the sailor Adumas, the richest and most populated of any along the Ogowè. The people are pleasant and quiet, and love the white man, from whom they learn some of the arts of civilised life; they have abolished slavery, which they once practised. The visit to this land was like an enchanting dream to Giacomo, who found more good in the natives than his brother Pietro had done. Here are the palms that yield oil, the banana, and the manioc. Cheerful villages surrounded by circles of green trees are near each other along the banks of the river, and in the distance are mountains covered with forest. It seemed a park in an Oriental garden, the view changing at every point—the tints now misty, now clear in the vivid light of a tropical sun shining on a warm and humid atmosphere.

But Giacomo, who had left Pecile at a station behind, could not remain among the Adumas. 'I must say farewell to this enchanted land, the air of which is filled with the sweet perfumes of the orchids and tree mimosa, and where it seems that one might live for ever.' He arrived at Franceville, the French station on the Ogowè, and there began to make collections of insects, fish, birds, reptiles, and mammalia; to study geology and botany; and, as a recreation, to take photographs.

He also made ethnographic collections, and studied the natives in their daily life. He observed the texture of their stuffs, their cooking, their work in clay and in iron, their tattooing, and their modes of burial. Geology was the most difficult of these studies, as vegetation in Central Africa covers the ground with a thick mantle, as if it would hide the earth from which it draws its beauty. It is rare to find an exposure of the rocks, and often the only way to study them is by examining the stones in the beds of the streams.

GIACOMO DI BRAZZA.

CHAPTER XIII.

GIACOMO DI BRAZZA, ATTILIO PECILE, AND
PIETRO ANTONELLI.

GIACOMO DI BRAZZA and Pecile, like Pietro di Brazza, crossed from the sources of the Ogowè to those of the Alima on foot through the land of the Batékès. Here the land looks sterile and desolate, contrasting sadly with the wealth of vegetation and the lovely scenery of the Lower Ogowè, and of the Alima or the Congo. All is changed—the earth, the vegetation, the form of the houses, the inhabitants, the customs, and the climate.

Gentle undulations of the ground rise one after the other, covered with quartz sand, upon which grows low and stunted grass. But the patient labour of the people—especially of the women—has its reward. Their villages on the summits of the low hills are hidden in clumps of planted trees, under which grow all things necessary for subsistence. The Batékès are an industrious people, and easily become burden-bearers to the Congo, by way of the Alima, or to the Ogowè. Our explorers, following mainly in the steps of Pietro di Brazza, but diverging to one side or the other up the tributary streams, where white men had never been, at last, after eight days of sailing in the long boats on the Alima, through dense dark walls of palm-trees, united by festoons of thick vines, came out upon the 'immense, imposing, majestic Congo.' 'A cry of surprise and admiration came from my men, the first sign to me that the black man feels the power of Nature's scenic grandeur. I let fall my compass and papers; the rowers stopped rowing and gazed in silence. We were all fascinated by this grand and unexpected scene. It was not a river before us, but a sea full of islands, covered with thick vegetation—islands ranged in long lines, bluish or dark, or white as snow from the sand. The sun in the zenith, veiled by the transparent vapours of noonday, without the smallest cloud, filled the sky with a white, uniform, dazzling light. It was as if the vapoury atmosphere had the light in itself, absorbing and multiplying that of the hidden sun.'

Too long would be the account of this remarkable journey of three years and a half, or the descriptions of natural scenery and of the customs of the natives. Giacomo went down the Congo to

Brazzaville, took part in the splendid reception given by the chief Makoko to Pietro, and then returned by the same route up the Congo and the Alima, and across land to the sources of the Ogowè, then down the Ogowè to Franceville and Madiville, another French station.

Having spent two years in these wilds, Giacomo and Pecile prepared to return to Italy, when unexpected events induced them to make another expedition by land to the tribes of the interior.

They went north-east, following the line of division between the waters of the Congo and the Ogowè, and discovering many new tributaries, as this part of Africa had never been explored.

After this they returned by the Alima and the Congo to the West African shore, and thence to Italy, where they were received by the Roman Geographical Society with honour. But the African fever had taken hold of Giacomo di Brazza, and in less than a year from his return he died in Rome at the early age of twenty-six, having already accomplished more than many older men.

The adventures of Attilio Pecile during this journey were almost identical with those of his friend, but he treated on his return chiefly of the character and origin of the tribes they had visited. On their second journey they penetrated to a populous region, which is the cradle of the cannibal tribe Baccali. But the two white men, although strangers, were generally treated not so much as equals and friends as superior beings. To this contributed their own peaceable manners and their humanity to their servants, to the old, the suffering, or those in peril. Once in passing through a deserted village they found a sick old woman without food who had been left behind alone. They could not remain with her, but they gave her a chicken, their only food for that day.

Once in the waters of the Alima, when a hippopotamus upset their boat and threw them into the water, Pecile caught hold of a sinking black and, swimming through the herd of hippopotami, brought him safe to land. Once, dressed in a loose cretonne costume of his own make, Pecile caught a large bird, and sitting down on a mat, with a circle of natives around him, took off the feathers. By giving the greater part of it to them he gained the reputation of being a most disinterested man. He wandered about from village to village in his flowered cretonne dress without weapons of any kind. If he sat down to write, with his ink held in a knot of wood, the children came about him and curiously touched his paper.

On the other side of Africa, where Assab, on the Bay of Assab, and the port of Zeila, on the Red Sea, and Massowah have attracted many Italians, Count Pietro Antonelli—a nephew of the cardinal so long Secretary of the Papacy—has spent many years.

Antonelli made his first visit to King Menilek in 1879, arriving in Shoa with an arm wounded by the accidental discharge of a pistol. The native doctors sent to him by Menilek tortured him to find the ball, until Antonelli lost faith and patience in them, and undertook himself the care of his wounds. When he went afterwards with Antinori to be presented to Menilek, he found the king seated on the threshold of a large cabin surrounded by his attendants. Menilek called for the boxes of Antonelli, and examined them one by one, turning out all the articles, and selecting for himself those which pleased him—a 'useful and agreeable occupation.'

COUNT PIETRO ANTONELLI.

To these articles Antonelli added as presents to the king some guns and pistols, and he found, in return, on leaving the royal premises, a magnificent mule in red harness. He also received from the king food on a princely scale during his visit. He describes the Shoa as an earthly paradise, with a fine climate, abundant food, and peaceable inhabitants. The fertility of the soil is prodigious, as there are two or even three harvests in the year. The people cultivate little, but gather in much.

The rural implements are imperfect; the plough is only an iron point dragged lightly over the ground by the oxen, and there is no spade.

The Abyssinian farmer can work only 117 days of the year, as the other 248 are festivals, which, if he did not observe, his land would be confiscated by the priest.

Antonelli spent much time at Let-Marifià, and made several journeys over the desert between Shoa and the Red Sea. He often visited Menilek, and became a favourite at court, and his influence in discouraging the slave-trade was important.

The enmity of Mohammed Anfari, chief of the savage Danakili, who killed Bianchi and Giulietti, is said to have been caused by the delay of a caravan of slaves which had been detained by Menilek at the suggestion of Antonelli.

He, together with Dr. Traversi, followed Menilek to his wars with the Gallas. They encamped on the Lake Zuai, and afterwards on the highland of Albassò, all territory lately conquered by Menilek.

During the war between Italy and Abyssinia Antonelli acted as diplomatic counsellor to Menilek, with whom he was in high favour; and it may be to his counsels that Menilek is indebted for the enlargement to the south of his kingdom, and for the possession of Abyssinia after the death of Negus John. Menilek is now King of Ethiopia, and calls himself the king of kings, the lion of the tribe of Judah, the descendant of the Queen of Sheba. With 2000 guns procured for him by Antonelli from the Italian Government, he conquered the negroes and the savage tribes of

Galla, Ghèra, Goggiam, and Tigrè. Far from opposing the colonial policy of Italy in Africa, and the occupation of Massowah, Saati, Keren, and Asmara, he has formed an alliance with, and asked for the protection and friendship of, Italy. The embassy which he sent in August to Italy under the escort of Count Antonelli consisted of eight persons of rank and thirty soldiers and servants.

The gifts of Menilek to the king and the government were a young elephant, mules and gazelles, sixty ivory tusks, each a yard in length; a gold head-dress, wrought as exquisitely as the old Etruscan jewellery, of which there are so many specimens in the museums of Italy, and his own royal robe, diadem, and sceptre.

Prince Makonnen, the ambassador, who is a relative of Menilek, was received on board the ship at Naples by Count Salimbeni, who was at the time of the battle of Dogali a prisoner of King John at Asmara.

When the embassy arrived in Rome, hearing that the father of Antonelli had just died, they went to the cemetery Campo Verano, to pray at the grave, and showed the greatest sympathy and affection to their friend. Makonnen is thirty-five years old, tall and straight and thin; the head long, the features fine, like those of a European. He was received by King Humbert in the hall of the throne at the Quirinal Palace at Rome, with the usual ceremony for the reception of ambassadors. Troops were stationed along the streets near the Quirinal and in front of the palace. The crowd along the streets applauded and cried, 'Long life to our allies!' The dresses worn by the ambassador and his suite were all of brilliant-coloured silk, embroidered with gold and silver thread. They wore turbans and large white mantles, beneath which could be seen their shining scimitars and shields. Makonnen bowed three times to the earth before King Humbert, who was seated gravely on the throne, under the red velvet canopy, and wore the brass helmet with white plumes of a general. But when the king left the throne, and the state which he rarely assumes, and descended with his natural, easy manner to shake hands with all of the embassy, they were enchanted. 'Oh! your king,' said Makonnen afterwards, 'your king is wonderful!'

The chief merit of this alliance with the powerful sovereign of Ethiopia is due to Antonelli. He has been replaced at the court of Menilek by Count Salimbeni, but has been sent on a special mission to Ethiopia by the Italian Government.

CHAPTER XIV.

GIUSEPPE HAIMANN AND GIACOMO BOVE.

GIUSEPPE HAIMANN made a journey in 1882 to Cyrene, sent out by the Milan Commercial Exploration Society in Africa.

He was accompanied by his courageous and accomplished wife, Angela Bettoni Haimann. They were prepared also several years later to accompany the expedition of Gustavus Bianchi to Abyssinia, but owing to the danger, especially for a woman, of travelling in that region they were dissuaded from going by the Italian Geographical Society.

Mr. Haimann took part in the famous five days' patriotic resistance made in 1848 by the Milanese against the tyranny of the Austrians. He filled with honour various public legal offices, during many years, and passed five years of his life at Cairo in the Ministry of Justice. His journey through Cyrene was made at this time, and the account of it, republished in book form after his death in 1883 by his widow, is extremely interesting.

Although Cyrene is not an unexplored country, and is near to Italy, it is rarely visited by Italians, and is almost as unknown to them as Australia or New

Zealand. Yet in ancient times that region, as well as all the African coast of the Mediterranean, was subject to Rome and in active commercial relations with her. The horses of Cyrene ran in the circuses of the Eternal City, and the men were celebrated for their skill as charioteers in the races. Its perfumes were sought by the Roman matrons, and one of its plants was counted a remedy against every ill. Now it is depopulated and reduced to misery; forgotten by the modern civilised nations, and the ruins of ancient palaces and fortresses alone prove how flourishing and populous it was.

In ancient times Cyrene was celebrated for its fertility and wealth. It produced grain, oil, honey, horses, and sheep. Herodotus says, 'The territory of Cyrene, the highest of Libya, has three seasons. The abundant harvest along the coast is scarcely gathered when that of the hills is mature, and after that comes the harvest of the highest region, so that the people are occupied eight months of the year in gathering the fruit and grain.'

From the exaggerated perils of travelling in the interior, Cyrene, although so near to Egypt, has been little visited of late years.

Before going with his wife on the two months' excursion to Cyrene, Mr. Haimann visited George Schweinfurth at Cairo. 'Why,' said that distinguished traveller, 'do you Italians not think more of Cyrene? You could found agricultural and manufacturing establishments there. The ground is rich; the rains in winter compensate for the droughts in summer; there are forests of olives, cypress and every sort of wood; there are natural ports, in one of which the entire French fleet once took refuge. From thence is the easiest and most direct access to Central Africa. The interior of the country, once the seat of flourishing Greek civilisation, now almost deserted except by wandering Bedouins, yields little to the Ottoman Government, which would readily permit colonisation. The Italians might construct a railroad to Egypt, and thus make sure of the shortest route to India, which they are in danger of losing when Austria extends her roads to the Ægean Sea.'

This advice struck Haimann as a revelation, and from that time the journey to Cyrene was to him a patriotic labour. Moved by Schweinfurth's counsel, President Camperio, of the African Exploration Society at Milan, also visited Cyrene at the same time, but travelling in another direction from Mr. and Mrs. Haimann. Before reaching Bengasi the travellers were shipwrecked on the coast, and entered the principal city of Cyrene in a forlorn plight.

But in a few days they organised a small caravan of seven camels, with mules for themselves, and guides, drivers, and servants.

Sidi Muftah, the leader of the caravan, said in Bedouin fashion in taking charge of them, 'My life and that of my family and of all my tribe are dedicated to you. Woe to them who touch a hair of your heads.'

He was a tall, athletic, and finely-proportioned man. He rode a beautiful dark Arab horse, and employed his intervals of leisure in sewing garments for his wife and black slave.

Not far from Bengasi they passed a cavern with a lake, believed to be the ancient Lethe, into which the Greeks imagined that the souls of the departed were immersed, to make them forget all their past sins before entering the Elysian Fields.

They were threatened by a band of Bedouins, who, however, only feigned an assault, and left them frightened, but not hurt. They passed several ruins of fortresses and palaces, and reached at length the site of the ancient city of Cyrene, but could not remain there long enough to explore its interesting ruins.

·Mrs. Haimann visited a harem, spending a whole afternoon with the women, to whom she presented some Roman pearls.

After two months of this life—sleeping in tents, meeting caravans of Bedouins, gathering botanical and zoological treasures, and making the tour of the peninsula—they returned, not without regret, to the habits and comforts of civilised Europe.

Giacomo Bove died tragically by his own hand in 1887 at Verona, having taken the African fever on the Congo the year before. He returned sick from a journey made in Equatorial Africa, where he had been sent by the Ministry of Foreign Affairs, to examine the Congo river and report what prospect there would be for Italian commerce. The fever contracted there continued in Italy, depressing his spirit as well as weakening his body. He saw everything dark and melancholy, and finally took his own life in a moment of mental aberration at the age of thirty-five. He was a distinguished naval officer, in 1873 making a voyage to China and Japan, and in 1878 going with Baron Nordenskjöld on board the Vega to the North Sea. On his return he gave an interesting lecture before the Roman Geographical Society, which showed thorough acquaintance with Arctic explorations. He then projected an expedition to explore the Antarctic Ocean, and succeeded in making a preparatory voyage to Tierra del Fuego. But the large sum of money necessary for such an important undertaking was not collected, and Bove was obliged to abandon that idea.

He who had dreamed of struggling with the icebergs and discovering the unknown lands of the Antarctic region accepted the mission to Congo, where the heat, the miasms, the long journeys on foot through pathless forests, overcame him.

Travelling and seeing the wonders of the world was a necessity to the bold nature of this explorer. With another Italian, Captain Fabrello, he set out eagerly for the Congo, and before arriving at its mouth enjoyed the view of all the ports on the western coast of Africa.

He landed at the Canaries, Sierra Leone, Liberia, Accra, Quittà, Lagos, Fernando Po, Gaboon, and many settlements between the mouths of the Ogowè, the Niger, and the Congo. He notes the progress of Mahommedanism in that part of Africa, and the predominant influence there of England, France, and Germany, leaving little room for that of Italy. The Niger, he says, is the principal artery of Africa, and the railroad built by France between the Niger and the Senegal will injure the commerce of the Mediterranean.

Bove and Fabrello visited the King of Old Calabar in the city of Duke, at the delta of the Niger. King Orok received them stretched upon an old sofa in an unkingly position. He is hated by the other chiefs, and his palace was burned down the year before, notwithstanding the human skull hung at the door to save him from misfortune. He now rarely immolates human victims at the funerals of great persons, or on solemn occasions, having been persuaded by the Protestant missionaries not to do so, but his tender mercies even are cruel, and the city of Duke abounds with persons destitute of nose, eyes, or ears. At the Bay of Banana their ship cast anchor in the waters of the Congo, which push out sixty miles into the ocean. They visited all the farms and establishments on the Lower Congo, but were detained by the rains from continuing their journey to the upper part of the river. The caravan of the expedition consisted of ninety-five natives, who were encamped on the banks of a confluent of the great river, waiting until the waters subsided to proceed by short journeys on foot from Matadi to Stanley Pool, where Bove and Fabrello took the steamer up the river. Bove was disappointed in the size of the Congo river, which he considered less magnificent than the rivers of Siberia and South America.

'Lower Congo,' he says, 'is not a beautiful country. The vegetation is not rich; the shores are not thickly populated; the flora and the fauna are poor.'

The road from Matadi to Lucungu he found monotonous and scarce of animal life. Limited views, yellow hills, deep and dark valleys, rivers and torrents hidden between high, inaccessible rocks, roads that climb nude, rocky mountains, few groups of trees, and sun all day long were all that he saw in that much vaunted region.

The grass grew so high in the plains that they walked sometimes in a sort of tunnel, and in the valleys, instead of grass, grew reeds fifteen feet high, where it was no rare thing to meet unexpectedly an elephant or a buffalo. The villages are at two or three hours' distance from each other, and generally consist of four or five huts with small gardens. Water is always found at a distance, and is carried in large gourds by the women, who do that and all the other hard work, while the men sit idle all day, and only climb the date trees at evening to get the delicious sap which makes wine. After many days of long and tiresome marching the Italian mission reached Leopoldville, the central station between Upper and Lower Congo. It is situated at the opening of the lake or pool formed by the Congo river, and is surrounded by a fertile plain covered with luxuriant vegetation. Bove's journey was continued in the steamers up the river, but the fever which attacked him about this time rendered him incapable of further service, and in the following year caused his death in Italy.

LUIGI ROBECCHI BRICCHETTI.

CHAPTER XV.

LUIGI ROBECCHI BRICCHETTI'S JOURNEY ACROSS LIBYA.

THE Engineer Luigi Robecchi Bricchetti is one of the most energetic and daring of the Italian explorers in Africa. His journey over the Libyan desert to the Oasis of Jupiter Ammon, although not made in an undiscovered region, exposed him to great dangers, privations, and sufferings. Few travellers would have had courage to start as he did in 1885, from Alexandria in Egypt, with four camels, the driver, and two servants; adapting himself to the habits, food, and dress of the Bedouins among whom he journeyed. But the charm of the desert repaid him for all. The wild life of the Bedouins seemed to him at times more desirable than the habits of civilised countries, yet the dazzling splendour of Africa, the mist of the desert, the golden sunsets and friendly bivouacs with the Bedouins are obscured on his return by the comforts of his friend's house and a dish of warm strong broth. Even he, infatuated as he was, confesses that the land of pyramids, sphinxes, obelisks, and ophthalmia possesses none of the comforts of European life. The beauty of the sky, the purity of the air, and the serenity of lovely nights, are not sufficient to make one forget the burning sun, the insupportable heat and storms that raise whirlwinds of sand.

Even before reaching the desert he was impressed by the frightful monotony of the Egyptian country, so different from the variety of Italy. It is a vast plain, sometimes covered with water, sometimes a marsh, or carpeted with verdure, or a sandy desert. Palms rise here and there, alone or in groups, and miserable villages with houses constructed of mud and straw give an aspect of permanent ruin. The manners of the Arab people contrast strangely with those of Europeans. They wear their clothes long and ample; they cut their hair and let the beard grow, they cover their heads in token of respect, and salute standing upright, and pass their lives seated. Their grave and austere aspect as they sit on the ground all day long meditating, is a great contrast to the active, joyous, energetic manner of Christian people.

The principal object of Robecchi's journey was

to explore the coast, and seek new roads for commerce with Italy in that region. But he was obliged to undertake it not only at his own expense, but at his own risk, as the Egyptians opposed it, and refused to sanction his expedition. The camel-driver and the two servants formed a trio worthy, he says, of 'being hung,' and the miserable camels not only upset his baggage, but hurt him with their hard trotting. But the driver sang their praises. There was, he said, a difference between camels, and these were light as gazelles, strong as lions, mild as lambs, and like the Arab horses their genealogy could be traced to the most noble and ancient sources. Not dismayed, however, Robecchi continued the march, sleeping at night on the sand, covered by a tent improvised from his drab mantle that he wore by day. Water is scarce, and when found at the wells along the way is often so dark, murky, and oily that he compares it to castor oil. The black servant from Siuwah at the Oasis of Jupiter Ammon who offered Robecchi this delectable fluid to drink could not understand the description of ice, when Robecchi with home-sick longing told him of this wonderful solid water hard as a rock, which melts in warmer water and cools it. The wells along the way give water of every mineral quality, which only thirst could induce the weary traveller to drink. The water is often also spoiled by the ablutions of the Bedouins, who after drinking wash themselves at the wells, without regard to those who come after them. Robecchi often visited the tents of these wandering Bedouins, who received him kindly, and would have offered hospitality if their extreme poverty had not prevented it. Their tents, or rather cabins, made of old worn straw mats drawn over four poles, were so small that they seemed intended rather for one person than for a family, and were incredibly filthy. They led him occasionally to wells constructed by the ancient Greeks and Romans, remarkable for size and perfection, which afforded delicious pure, cold water. One of these, three feet wide and ninety deep, was lined with stone, and the water was drawn up in a bucket or bag of sheep-skin attached to a rope pulled by a donkey running constantly backward and forward.

The tribe of the Senegrah, although nude and miserable, prefer their liberty to the comforts of a fixed habitation. Although dressed in rags, they are proud, and would not give their daughters to a rich farmer, to a merchant, or a Turkish soldier. Their way of life is simple. At early dawn they rise, milk the sheep, the goats, the camels, and the cows, make the butter and drink the thin milk that remains. The women not only care for their large families, but do nearly all the outdoor work. They raise the tents, grind the corn, gather the dry weeds and resinous plants for a fire, and weave stuff made of wool and camels' hair. Until they are twenty years old these women have an ideal perfection of form, but after that, hard labour makes them quickly grow old and ugly. They wear a long white cotton dress, drawn in at the waist, tattoo the chin, the arms, and the hands, and tinge the nails red. They are tall and well-proportioned, with fine regular features, a noble, grave, majestic air, and bright dark eyes veiled by long lashes. But their fate is hard. Robecchi saw one of them walking over the stones of the desert with a bundle on her head, a child on her right shoulder, another hidden in the folds of her dress and tugging at her breast, another in her left arm, while the husband rode placidly ahead on his mule.

Women were always considered inferior beings by these people, who yet preserve the habits, superstitions, and ideas of their ancestors. They believe in magic and metempsychosis, and consider robbery almost a domestic occupation. Yet many of the tribes have noble and generous traits of character, and preserve the ancient beautiful simplicity of patriarchal life. They love the desert, and rarely consent to live in cities. They need little, and the desert heat does not injure them. They are strong, and can endure fatigue; a small cake of flour, a few olives or dates, are sufficient to revive them after a day's march. At night they need no roof or tent, and stretch themselves on the sand with their sack for a pillow, reviving like summer flowers with the night dew that is fatal to Europeans. The true Bedouin is free, and bows servilely to no man. He enters without ceremony into the palace of a great man, and speaks to him as he would to an equal. They have a passion for story-telling, and often at evening seated in a circle near their tents listen to one who begins a story about genii and fairies, with the traditional words, 'Once upon a time there was—.'

The road to the Oasis of Jupiter Ammon after

following the coast turns off to traverse the desert. Robecchi saw before him an interminable plain ruffled by the sand, like waves of the sea; where there was no trace of the footsteps of man or beast, no trees, no streams, no harvests, no lowing of herds or song of birds; nothing but sterility, silence, and death.

Life in these burning deserts becomes a burden; the mind cannot act; conversation is an effort, and time is precious. 'Every one for himself, and God for all,' is the theory of the desert. If one falls sick, he is left behind; if two caravans meet, they waste no time together, but murmur, as the camels pass with their regular gait, the usual benediction, 'May Mahomet guide and protect you, and conduct you to your homes with the mercy and benediction of God!' But although the road was long and difficult, the sun burning like red-hot iron, the refraction of light from the sand dazzling his eyes, and water far away, Robecchi enjoyed the desert life. 'I shall never forget those days,' he says. 'They were the best of all my life. Seated on my camel, whistling and singing my old songs, I went on at the head of my little caravan, happy under the hot sun and enjoying the solitude of the desert. Although destitute of luxuries, I did not complain, but felt new life in my veins. I learned to love the land without verdure, those paths improvised among the rocks. Sleeping on the bare sand, under the shadow of a rock, with the stars above, waking by night when scorpions or ants ran over me, and always on my feet at dawn of day, this life had its own charm of independence and liberty.'

But it was not so delightful when they lost their way, and came near dying of thirst and despair. Then, like a lovely mirage, he saw his own dear distant country, and the friends who would long expect in vain his return from that burning land. When after being lost four hours they at last found the road, they went on all day, eating almost nothing, in order not to arouse the terrible thirst which they had so little water to assuage. They could not even sleep when night came on, for fear of dying in the sand, but kept marching on, worn and weak as they were. Sad and mute, with the tongue stuck to the palate, and a burning in the throat and stomach, they passed through the volcanic mountains, where the rays of the sun seemed to fall like floods of light. They had no more water, and the heat and weariness made them almost wild. Finally they descried two trees, and farther on the Oasis of Gharah, which meant salvation for them and life. The inhabitants, at first hostile to Robecchi, gradually became friendly, accepted his gifts of sugar to the children and medicines to the adults, for which they exchanged baskets of exquisite dates, and at evening danced and sang for his amusement.

One month after leaving Alexandria he reached the Oasis of Jupiter Ammon, or Siuwah, one of those green spots in the vast expanse of sand and rock called by the ancients the 'Isles of the Fortunate,' as if it were a special favour of the gods to live there. But the songs of the poets who admired the palm and olive trees, the gardens, and wells, and streams could not hide the real loneliness of the oases, where Pharaohs and emperors sent their enemies to die of grief and home-sickness.

Few strangers in modern times have entered the city of Siuwah, and Robecchi risked his life in doing so without recommendations of any kind to the governor. Dressed as a Bedouin, brown and travel-worn, he was mistaken at first for one of the inhabitants, and went to the house of his servant, where he threw himself down to sleep on a mat in the court. At midnight he was aroused by a noisy crowd that surrounded him, throwing the light of their torches on his face and disputing with his servant. While he slept an earthquake had alarmed them, the whole blame of which they attributed to the presence of the Christian in their city. He readily took the advice of his servant, and went out of the city limits, presenting himself next day to the governor, and winning his sympathy and protection.

The population of the Oasis of Siuwah is about 6000. It consists of two races differing in character and also in religion, part of them being Senussians and part Mahdists. On this oasis existed in ancient times the temple of Jupiter Ammon, which had a world-wide fame. Those persons were accounted purified who at least once in their lives went to visit the celebrated oracle. Robecchi saw the ruins of this once splendid temple, which was visited until the last days of the Roman empire. Now there are only stones fallen one over the other, a few broken white marble columns buried under the sand, and the ruins of the principal entrance. By stealth and at night Robecchi visited the ancient necropolis near the temple, which holds about 80,000 mummies, laid so close together as to occupy small space, and now thickly encrusted with saline material. He succeeded in bringing away in a sack and at great risk to his life, thirty skulls, which are now in the National Museum at Florence; a valuable addition to our knowledge of these ancient races.

The town of Siuwah is a network of fantastic zigzag streets, the houses without visible windows; the upper rooms built across the streets, so that even in the day-time Robecchi saw people groping about in the dark and dirty lanes below with lanterns. The air within and without these habitations is pestilential from the exhalations of every kind of refuse. A stream of dirty water often runs over into the streets, saturating the soil and leaving a black scum upon the surface.

In contrast with this vileness of man are the lovely gardens and woods, where vigorous Nature practises all her enchantments. The Arab, used to desert lands beaten by the sun, regards a luxuriant vegetation—the shade of the palm and olive trees, the running of water, the thick twining of rose bushes—as the greatest wonder of Nature.

The gardens which are so numerous in the Oasis of Siuwah do not in the least resemble those of Europe, with their symmetrical walks and studied rows of flowers.

Fruit trees irregularly planted grow low near the ground, and mix their branches together. The date, the olive, the lemon, the fig, the pomegranate, mingle the odour of their blossoms with the fragrance of roses and other flowers. This wild charm of Nature renders these gardens of the oasis poetical and delicious.

Notwithstanding the superstition, the filthiness, and idleness of the people of Siuwah, Robecchi lingered, studying their language, character, and ideas, until the governor for a slight offence told him to leave.

'I left with pain that happy island, where I had experienced such sad and joyful emotions; where I had felt infinite beatitude and agonies of fear. There I had felt the tie which unites man to earth; there I had contracted friendships and awakened hatred. I had grown accustomed to those strange people, and left in that legendary oasis a part of my heart, when I remembered that I should never return there.' Sufferings from fever, thirst, and famine, and the loss of several camels almost reduced him to despair on the return over the desert, but he reached Alexandria at last, glad to lay aside his Bedouin costume, and sleep in a bed instead of on the sand with the stars above him.

Three years later, in 1888, Robecchi visited the city of Harar, already known to travellers, and on the road to which Count Porrò and his companions were killed by the Somali. Starting from the coast at Zeila, but taking a more southerly direction than the road which leads over the Isa-Somali country to Shoa, with five camels, a driver, and three servants, he reached Harar, but not without some danger. He was stopped at Artu, the place where Porrò and Cocastelli were murdered, by a number of Somali, who, knowing that he was an Italian, insisted that he should give them news of the natives arrested at that time. He showed them his arms, and hastened on to Gialdessa, three hours' journey, where he learned next day that about fifty of the Somali had sworn to take his life that night, if he had remained at Artu. The Governor or Degiac Makonmen, cousin of King Menilek, received Robecchi courteously, and gave him a commission to build an Abyssinian church in Harar according to his own design, and to direct the labours of about 200 very dirty soldiers who were erecting another smaller church. When this was completed he persuaded the Degiac to lay the corner-stone with ceremony.

He prepared the stone with several mottoes in Arabic scratched on the surface, and in the presence of the priest and about 1000 other persons went through with some ceremonies calculated to impress them.

While in Harar Robecchi occupied his time also in long and patient study of the Somali language, making a vocabulary, which, now that Italy through her friend Menilek has acquired more influence in that region, will be useful to travellers. No translation, he says, has yet been made of the Bible into the Somali language, although Cardinal Massaja prepared a grammar and vocabulary of the Galla. The Harar language is of Semitic origin; the Somali, and the Galla are spoken in the Somali peninsula; and the meaning of the same word in all three languages was gathered by Robecchi from the mouths of the people.

The race of the Somali have no resemblance to the negro races. Although savages they are intelligent, and their faces and forms are beautiful. They are shepherds and merchants, but idle, and are born and grow old in rags. The Somali never forgets that he is a free son of the desert. He is proud of the number of enemies he has killed, and the death of a native gives him the right to wear in his hair for one year a large black feather, or a white one when he has killed a lion or a European.

The road from Zeila to Harar, once so perilous to Italians, is now safe, if made in company and under the protection of a caravan leader. The distance is 250 miles, which is accomplished in fifteen or twenty days, although the couriers do it sometimes in five or six days. These couriers of the Isa-Somali are tall, black, and thin. They carry nothing with them but the lance and shield, a goat-skin bottle of water, a bag filled with dry bread, and the letters wrapped in linen. Bareheaded and barefooted, they run all day under the torrid sun over the sand or the volcanic rocks. The road from Gialdessa to Harar is mountainous, with beautiful views here and there, when it is not through narrow defiles. The traveller at last sees the city of Harar built upon a hill, with a wall twelve or fifteen feet high. The brownish-red tint of the houses and wall, the plantations of coffee, and gardens of bananas, the three white minarets, and the sycamores give it a fantastic and almost magical appearance. It is the largest city of Eastern Africa, and the purity of the air and mildness of the climate make it a delightful place.

It has 40,000 inhabitants, and now pays tribute to Menilek. Much capital now lying idle in Italy might be used there in commerce to advantage. Robecchi succeeded in obtaining here, as he did in Siuwah, thirty skulls of the natives, but with even more difficulty and danger than there.

The women wear more jewellery than clothes, and delight in moving about to make their bells and bracelets heard. On the arms they wear half-a-dozen iron bracelets that weigh several pounds, besides armlets of brass, bone, and tin. They wear also rings on their fingers, in their noses, and on the upper part of the ear, besides necklaces of beads, shells, and bits of brass.

In 1890 Robecchi made an exploration from Obbia to Allula, on the Somali coast, which elicited the warm praise of the traveller Schweinfurth, who writes to him: 'You can now cover with a hundred names a part still blank on the map of Africa; a new proof that to make discoveries and find dangers it is not always necessary to go to the centre of the continent.'

The Italian protectorate over Obbia is now acknowledged, and the Sultan Jusuf Ali being friendly to Robecchi, sought to dissuade him from making the journey in the interior, which even he considered dangerous. But Robecchi set out with six men and five camels, finding after six days' march a tribe friendly to the Italians. On the eighth night he was attacked by a horde of savages, who soon retired on hearing the guns. They robbed him, however, of his horse and of the only extra pair of shoes, so that the rest of the journey was made on foot. 'It was not easy,' he writes, 'but I am used to it.'

On horseback and on foot he traversed 600 miles in this journey, opening new roads to commerce, and proving himself one of the most courageous and useful travellers of Italy.

CHAPTER XVI.

GAETANO CASATI.

MAJOR GAETANO CASATI was born in 1838 at Lesmo, a beautiful town in the hilly region of Brianza, near Milan. He took part in the war of independence against Austria in 1859, and then as a Captain of Bersaglieri fought the brigands in Southern Italy for eleven years. In 1866 he took part in the fourth and last campaign for Italian independence, and then was occupied in the Institute at Leghorn for the construction of the Military Map of Italy. He was promoted to the rank of major, and might have continued a brilliant military career if another ideal had not induced him in 1879 to offer his resignation from the army. Africa beckoned him away from Italy. He would know the secrets of the Upper Nile; he would see the strange inhabitants of those unexplored regions, and find the Akkà, the chimpanzee and the silver-grey parrot. Under a calm exterior Casati hid an enthusiastic and adventurous nature, rare energy and courage, and an iron force of will. He was therefore the person adapted to aid Romolo Gessi in constructing maps of the Bar-Ghasal, where that marvellous soldier had just subdued Suleiman Bey. He was ready to start on the morrow, with just money enough to take him from Genoa to Suakim, and across the desert to Khartoum. After a month's journey in the Egyptian steamer up the Nile, he reached Gessi Pasha, who received him more as a dear relative than a subordinate officer, and nursed him through a violent fever which followed immediately.

Gessi left for Khartoum after one month and a half spent thus together, on that fatal journey when his ship, the Safia, was locked for months in the arms of aquatic plants in the River of the Gazelles, and 500 of his people died from famine, as he himself also did on arriving at Suez. Casati then for years explored Central Africa alone, without means, without an escort, and living like the natives, until he was called by Emin, Egyptian Governor of Southern Soudan, to aid him against the troops of the Mahdi. A great part of the notes of Emin to European journals on the flora and fauna of Central Africa, and the customs and history of the tribes there, were communicated to him by Casati. Extraordinarily modest, this Italian explorer speaks so little of himself in the *Ten Years in Equatorial Africa*, written on his return, that the story in many parts suffers for want of the central figure.

The notes of several years were destroyed by the cruel King Ciua or Cabrega, when he condemned Casati to death. Five months were lost at Zanzibar and Cairo on his return, in assisting his friend Emin, and trying to obtain for him back pay from the Egyptian Government. Yet, with all these disadvantages, Casati's descriptions of those ten years in Equatoria are thrilling. He had no need of written notes to remember hunger that lasted days and months, marches through bogs and virgin forests, imprisonment, escape from a horrible death, flight, and daily contact with races of black cannibals.

How strange the high ideals of the white man must have seemed to these, his only companions, with whom, as he knew several of their languages, he could converse freely! Casati was a 'strange man' to Emin, and even Stanley was surprised at an instance of his self-sacrifice, when sick with fever he refused to ask the liberated slaves to build him a hut of leaves and bark, because 'he would not have them think they had gone back to slavery.' Casati was the counsellor of Emin at Ladò and Wadelay on the Nile, in the long resistance made with a few Egyptian soldiers to the rebellious Soudanese troops of the Mahdi, who drove them continually further south. His name is now connected with those of Stanley and of Emin.

For one year after Casati separated from Gessi on the Bar-Ghasal nothing was heard from him. Then came a letter. Then another year of silence and another letter; and from 1883 to 1886, three years, not a word was heard from him nor from Emin, whom he had joined at Ladò.

He made long and difficult explorations in Niam-Niam, in Mambettù, in Unioro, in Bamba, and found the grave of Miani at Tangasi, under the famous tamarind tree; studied the course of the

River Uelle; visited the Sultan Mambanga; was taken prisoner and condemned to death by the Sultan Ciua; escaped to Bakangoi, crossed Mambettù. and found refuge with Emin Pasha at Ladò.

This long silence, and the fact that they were in between the Soudanese and cruel, ferocious tribes of savages, excited the compassion of the world. A relief expedition under the command of Stanley was organised. The relief funds collected for Emin were also for the liberation of Casati, and Stanley on leaving Italy for his adventurous journey said, 'I go as much for Casati as for Emin.' The Italians naturally thought chiefly of him. The African Exploration Society of Milan received subscriptions for him, and Giacomo Brazzà and Attilio Pecile, on their return from the Ogowè and the Congo, offered their rare collections to the government for a sum of money destined to the relief of Casati.

The long silence which followed Stanley's entrance into the wilds of the Dark Continent, no word coming from him, or from Emin, or Casati, seemed ominous of disaster. They were all mourned as lost or dead, and tidings of their dreadful end were daily expected. But the cloud lifted, and their return to the civilized world was expected with joy. Such an ovation was offered to Casati and to Emin by emperors, kings, queens, and governments as was never before received by any travellers. They, with the garrison of Ladò, including women and children, passed on foot through dark forests, and over high mountains, crossed new rivers, found new lakes, and saw at last the cross on the steeple, and enjoyed all the delights and comforts of civilised life.

Casati, worn out with the fatigues of the journey and a severe illness on the way, received at Zanzibar the congratulations of the Roman Geographical Society, which offered to pay the expenses of his return to Italy. He was greeted as a brother returned from the dead, one lost and found. He was met at Naples by a deputation from Rome, who boarded the ship when it landed. A banquet was given him at Naples, and another at Rome, and at Rome also a reception by the Geographical Society, to which 1000 persons were invited. But Casati modestly disclaimed these honours, and as soon as possible retired to the little Villa Giovio at Monza, to write down without notes what his memory retained of his adventures.

One of the first pictures of the Nile he gives is the scene at Cava, the great slave emporium above Khartoum. The river here is wide and tortuous, the water thick with earth, which forms islands in the stream, and arms and indentures on the shores. Here, some time after, the Mahdi barred the Nile with trees and stones to prevent navigation, but when Casati passed he was figuring as a great saint on the island Aba, almost in front of Cava. The wonderful fertility of the tropics is displayed upon this island and on the shores of the Nile. Palms and tamarind-trees, the mimosa, the acacia, and the papyrus grow there. There are wide fields and orchards; and in the forests antelopes, lions, and leopards, and pythons that wind their long bodies around the trees with the head looking out above. The whistle of the engine and slowing of the steamer at Aba gave the captain, the men, and most of the passengers an opportunity to pray with their faces turned to the island.

They were saluting with great veneration the future Mahdi—Mohammed Ahmed—who soon after caused such mourning in the Soudan. They believed him immortal, and said that once, 700 years ago, he had been translated to heaven, and had returned. Even the government paid him respect, and forbade wood for the vessels to be cut on that island. One of the officers gave an account to Casati of a visit he and others made to Mohammed Ahmed, who performed a miracle in their presence. Two jars full of milk and sugared water were passed round to forty persons, all of whom drank, and yet the liquid in the jars was not in the least diminished.

Two hours farther up the Nile the vessel entered the River of the Gazelles, Bar-Ghasal, a narrow river filled with long aquatic plants. The shores are marshy, and it is a desolate-looking country, without trees, and little inhabited. By day wasps torment the traveller, and by night innumerable mosquitos. In the river are groups of hippopotami, who with their heads out of the water watch the vessel with curiosity. Here Casati experienced the difficulty of navigating in the midst of the aquatic plants, which, tied from shore to shore, often stopped the vessel until cut with hatchets. He warned Romolo Gessi of this danger, and advised him to return to Khartoum by way of Ladò, farther up the Nile; but Gessi persisted in taking this route to Khartoum, and lost his life. Sixty-six times in seventeen days, says Casati, their vessel was stopped by these plants.

The patience and activity of the negroes who perform this labour are remarkable. The numerous tribes of the Dinca, all of one origin, but distinguished by a variety of customs and manners, are courageous in chasing wild beasts, but gentle and timid with strangers. Their limbs are agile and vigorous, they walk rapidly, and handle the lance and the bow with wonderful skill. Their habitations are huts made of straw with conic roofs. They wear goat-skins tied at the waist when they are not completely nude. They are a clean people, but sleep at night in beds of ashes, as a protection from the mosquitos and the changes of temperature, and in the morning look like walking spectres. They worship serpents, and keep one of these creatures, generally a python, in almost every house, feeding it with milk, allowing it to remain curled up in the house, and teaching it to answer when called. The Dincas loved Gessi because he liberated the slaves and punished the Arabs who carried on that infamous commerce.

Casati met Gessi at Wau, on the River Guir, crossing the stream filled with crocodiles in a canoe dug out of the trunk of a tree. The severe illness which followed detained Gessi until the crisis was past, and two days afterwards, at the door of the house, they gave each other the farewell kiss which was the last.

As soon as able, Casati left the station, now

commanded by another, with a few servants going towards the River Rohl, thus beginning that long exile in Africa which ended only in the tragic march with Stanley and Emin, from Unioro to Zanzibar. Fever accompanied him, so that he could not for some time make long journeys on foot. When near the borders of Macraca the chief sent him word not to enter that kingdom; and this caused him to begin a correspondence with Emin Bey, then at Ladò, on the Upper Nile. The tribe of the Abacà, on the contrary, received him kindly. They are a race of aborigines not fond either of labour or of war. The women add to their natural ugliness by inserting a large piece of ivory in the upper lip, and a smaller piece in the lower one, and sprinkling their bodies, first well greased, with a red powder procured by grinding the bark of a certain tree. They smoke in a long iron pipe, filling the cup when tobacco is scarce with hot coals alone, and smoking the tobacco only at intervals. They eat human flesh, but 'are neither inhuman nor ferocious.'

Crossing the River Dungù, Casati found himself in the province of Mambettù, where Schweinfurth, Miani, and Piaggia had preceded him. The wonderful things he had heard of that region, the splendid natural scenery, the mysterious River Uelle or Maqua, the streams so arched with trees that they seemed avenues, the banquets of human flesh, the pigmy population of the Akkà, or Tikki-Tikki, the lake seen by Piaggia—excited his curiosity. Here also at Tangasi he would visit the grave of Miani, the Italian explorer who died there. The river is famous for the number of crocodiles and hippopotami on the shores.

Casati was met by the chief Sunga, who offered him the use of some canoes, dug by the natives with fire and iron out of the trunk of an immense tree which is sometimes six feet in diameter. The King of Mambettù at his solemn banquets had the feast served in great tubs which required four men to move them, excavated in pieces of this wood.

He was invited by a chief to a meal consisting of crocodile meat cooked with leaves of manioca and bananas in palm oil, but the crocodile meat had so strong a smell of musk that he confined himself to the bananas.

The Monfù, a pigmy race in Mambettù, are blacker than the other races there. They are considered inferior, and are chased for slaves and the banquets of the chiefs. They are excellent agriculturists, strong, patient, and diligent, and the men assist the women in the labours of the field. They are not warlike, and use their weapons only for defence, cutting down trees along the roads when pursued. Casati saw twenty women of a tribe to the south brought in tied together by a rope, but to his great satisfaction they all escaped during the night.

At this time he heard that the Russian traveller, Dr. Junker, awaited him at the residence of Mambanga, the chief of the next tribe, and he was conducted to the dividing line of the kingdoms at war with each other by the chief Mabù. As he crossed alone he found Mambanga—tall, straight, agile, and bold—with a circle of his guards waiting to conduct him to Dr. Junker. The meeting of these two explorers, strangers to each other and of different nations, was like that of dear brothers who see each other after long absence. But they soon parted, taking different ways, Casati pushing on across the River Bomocandi, where the Sultan Azanga, after long consultation of the oracles, at last received him.

This African potentate is a cannibal, and absolute lord of the lives and limbs of his subjects. They swear by his foot, by his neck, by his shield; they crawl into his presence, they shout his praises, and salute when he sneezes. If, however, one of them should sneeze or cough before him, death might be the punishment. At his death the chief of this tribe is honoured by the immolation of human victims, selected from the principal men of the kingdom, and by the burying alive of his wives with his dead body.

Azanga, who is a tall and well-formed man, gave his hand to Casati, said he was glad to see him and retired, followed by blowing of trumpets and cries of admiration of the people. Whenever he goes out or re-enters, the trumpet blows, and the great horn at night announces that he has retired. 'Does the sun shine at Khartoum?' said Azanga one day to Casati. 'Certainly.' 'No, it cannot be, because this is the sun of my country, which is so large, and there are other kingdoms beyond mine. You inhabit another world.' 'As you will,' said Casati, 'but the sun is immense, and is placed in such a way that it can light your country and mine. I advise you not to discuss the power of the sun, as it might become offended and punish you.' The chief looked at him in silence with wide-open eyes, and laughed when Casati did, but rather convulsively. 'The flesh of the chimpanzee,' said Azanga, 'has no rival in delicacy;' and when Casati asked him what it resembled he answered, 'It is as good as human flesh.'

This benevolence of the sultan was changed to suspicion and cruelty by the re-inforcement of the garrison at the Egyptian station in the adjoining kingdom of his enemy, the chief Mambanga. Azanga demanded Casati's weapons, robbed him of his goods, and abandoned him to the vexations of the people. But the good offices of a brother of Azanga, to whom Casati fled, brought him to reason, and the traveller returned to Tangasi-Olòpo, the residence of Azanga being the limit of his pilgrimage in that direction.

In the valley of the Bomocandi, among the Niam-Niam, Casati found King Canna, a chief not so cruel as some of the others with whom he had made acquaintance. Canna made the compact of friendship with Casati, which is done by making a little wound in the arm of each with a knife and mixing the blood.

'Will you do me a favour?' he said one evening, when their conversation had been longer than usual. 'I wish to make the compact of friendship with you.' 'Yes, I will deny you nothing.' 'I thank you,' said Canna; 'I believed you would not, because you are always saying that you must leave me.' At dawn next day the courtiers, the women, the warriors, and the people gathered in the large court, and the exchange of blood took place to the beating of drums, and the frantic applause of the beholders, for Canna had obtained a great triumph in becoming the ally and the friend of the white men.

The king and his people remembered with affection Miani, and spoke with enthusiasm of his long beard and hair, and of the beautiful beads he gave them.

In 1883 Casati received an invitation from Dr. Edward Schnitzer, Emin Bey, to join him at Ladò on the Nile. After their meeting Emin accompanied Casati to Mambettù, visiting the stations and taking some soldiers with him. This aroused the opposition of many of the chiefs who had been friendly to Casati when he was alone, and Emin returned to Ladò, leaving his friend to continue explorations of the country. The progress of the Mahdi up the Nile and into Bar-Ghasal, and the cutting off the supplies of Ladò from Khartoum, soon recalled him to be the counsellor and aid of Emin.

He counselled Emin to defend himself at Gondokoro, and when his advice was not taken he wished to leave Soudan, returning alone by the difficult and dangerous way of Abyssinia. But the rebellion of the Egyptian garrison caused by the weak government of Emin and their fear of being abandoned to the cruelties of the savages, induced Casati to forget all irritations and sacrifice his own ideas to the safety and honour of his friend. He accepted the hard office of representing Emin with the King of Unioro, on Lake Albert, through whose kingdom Emin hoped to pass on the return to Europe from Wadelay, a station on the Upper Nile to which he had retired, leaving most of the troops at Ladò or Duflì.

Cabrega or Ciua, King of Unioro, a despotic, cruel, degraded tyrant, the enemy of all travellers and strangers, was then at war with his neighbour Muanga, King of Uganda. He desired the friendship of Emin, who had once visited him, in order to get possession of the ivory stored up at Wadelay, and have the benefit of the guns and ammunition of the Egyptian soldiers, to whom every other way of escape was closed.

Cabrega, a black man, 'timid, suspicious, tardy, irresolute, prejudiced, a liar, malicious, and cowardly,' was also superstitious and afraid of the evil eye. At the dawn of every day in a traditional attire, barefooted, he receives the compliments and congratulations of his relatives and of the people, who, to the sound of trumpets and drums, bow down to him and proclaim him 'absolute and powerful sovereign, beneficent father, dispenser of every good, and jealous custodian of the rights of the state.' His royal residence has seven doors, each of which is reserved for a special class of persons. One of these, leading to the most sumptuous and largest part of the palace, is for the members of the royal family, where they live, and where also the human sacrifices are made.

Cabrega formally received Casati in June, 1886. He was seated in a large chair, with his august feet resting upon a beautiful leopard skin. He wore a dress of fine cloth elegantly ornamented, and a red turban wound in Arab fashion around his head. Tall, and of colossal proportions, with a full expressive face and sarcastic smile, and a ready tongue, with graceful gesture Cabrega produces at first a not unfavourable impression. He listened quietly to the demands of the Governor of Soudan —that correspondence might pass freely; that peace should be made with Uganda, and that the Egyptian officers and soldiers should be allowed to retire that way to Egypt. But fears and suspicions afterwards assailed him, and he ended by making Casati a prisoner.

The savage king, being convinced that he had made a grave error in accepting the friendship of Emin, laid aside the mask, and in March, 1887, showed all his hatred of the white man. Casati was not allowed to leave his habitation, and was so guarded night and day that he could only with the greatest difficulty, by means of a friendly Arab merchant, communicate with Mr. Mackay, the missionary in Uganda. He employed a courageous Dinca boy, who came to his hut under pretence of selling goods, in helping him to receive nocturnal visits from his friends. After having made the guard destined to watch drunk, 'God pardon me,' says Casati, 'I received visits at night, and in this way knew all that was necessary for me, also all the scandals and quarrels of the royal house.'

Eight times in the course of the next few months Casati was disturbed at night by attacks upon his hut, made with the permission of the king, who hoped thus to get rid of an inconvenient witness or a supposed conspirator and enemy. He opposed to this treachery an appearance of indifference and a smiling face, as if nothing was the matter, but kept up a constant watch at night, taking his turn with the soldiers and servants in his company. One rainy night, when a boy kept watch, Casati, who slept badly from anxiety, got up and found the sentinel asleep. Shaking him vigorously, he heard the movement of a creature in flight only a few steps away, and next morning discovered that the boy's life had been saved by his vigilance, as the footsteps of a whole family of lions were found there. Cabrega, whose residence was three hours distant over a deserted road through marshes and reedy wilds, sent for Casati, to reproach him for the appearance of steamers sent by Emin to the Victoria Nile, and if possible get rid of him on the way home in the evening. He kept Casati waiting several hours, while the people passed in a long procession to gain a place of refuge, war having begun with Uganda. Armed men preceded the women and children, the slaves, the dogs, the goats, and the royal consorts, borne aloft on palanquins covered with ox-skins, and dressed in mantles of bright colours with strange designs. The crowd made way with cries of wonder and admiration as four strong men appeared carrying one of the fattened wives of Cabrega, an immense mass of flesh, with the eyes buried in their orbits. It is a custom at the courts of Unioro and Uganda, to fatten these women gradually by a special process until they can no longer walk, and are scarcely able even to crawl. Finally the king, seated on his large chair, with an angry countenance and twitching hands and feet, received Casati, and after a silence accused him of conspiring against Unioro, and of helping Emin to encroach upon its territory. The peril of Casati was extreme, but with extraordinary tact and courage he persuaded Cabrega that their only motive was to return to Zanzibar, and of his own peaceful intention. He even negotiated a peace for his inhospitable host with the invading chiefs of Uganda, when a word or motion of his hand would have rid him of the tormentor.

His own life was in danger at this time from Muanga of Uganda, who had given orders to kill him as well as Cabrega. He was only saved by the Christians of Uganda, whom the missionaries had told to protect him. Cabrega continued his policy of intrigue and treachery, anxious to prevent the passage of Emin and the troops through Unioro, and yet not bold enough to prevent it, or to kill Casati. Six boys of his tribe, who were at school at Wadelay, and would have been precious hostages for the life of Casati, were imprudently sent home by Emin. 'The remembrance of those days,' says Casati, ' even now, when I write, thrills me with fear.' Violence had taken the place of intrigue, and the wicked king and his wicked counsellors, not repressed by Emin, who seemed to have forgotten the perilous situation of his friend and ambassador, prepared to end the horrible drama. Emin was then powerless, having fled in the night from his soldiers, who threatened to make him prisoner. King Ciua-Cabrega was determined to be troubled no longer with the presence of the white man in his kingdom, and ordered the chief in whose charge he had given Casati to make away with him.

Gnacamatera, having failed in persuading Casati to go alone by night to him in order to seal the compact of friendship with blood, invited him with the Arab ivory merchant, Biri, kept also in a kind of imprisonment, to a meeting by day.

They started for the residence of the chief at six in the morning, and having crossed a torrent, found the ground filled with many armed men, who gathered around them as they passed. Not far off, at the foot of a large tree, was seated the high priest with a circle of the lesser magicians around. His head was covered by a rich turban of red stuff ornamented with beads and shells, and with two ox-horns on either side. In his left hand was a horn filled with magic powder, and he held in the right the conjuring stick. He wore a large mantle of ox-skin, and was seated in accordance with the dignity of his high office. The chief, a tall man, then came out, his coming being announced by the blowing of a trumpet, and the warriors, armed with guns, lances, shields, and bows and arrows, gathered around. Something important was evidently preparing, and Casati whispered to his companion—'God help us, all hope is vain, let us show courage!'

Ten minutes after the appearance of the chief, at a signal from him, the crowd of savages with horrible cries rushed upon Casati and his companions, tying them with ropes to the trees. Casati was barbarously tied by the throat, the arms, the wrists, the knees, and the ankles, and afterwards, to increase the torture, a rope was added around the waist. He was kept thus for hours, in the burning sun, subject to the scorn and derision of a bloodthirsty throng of 300 savages, while Gnacamatera went to search his house, believing he should find armed men there sent from Wadelay to conquer the kingdom of Cabrega. 'If I find them,' said the chief, 'you will be immediately killed.' He found nothing of the kind, of course, but destroyed the notes of Casati's journey—an irreparable loss. Casati in the meantime, tortured by the ropes and the heat and thirst, encouraged his companions, and even in that condition frightened the drunken fanatical mob.

When one of the boldest drew near and began to unloose the string of his shoe, probably to steal it, the prisoner gave such a cry of anger and disdain that the whole mass, taken with sudden fear, retreated from him like a wave of the sea falling over each other. They kept a respectful distance until one of the chiefs, in whom duty triumphed over fear, advanced cautiously, searched the pockets of their victim and reassured them that the bit of paper which they considered a charm was not there. Casati could not refrain from laughing at this, and his laugh was returned by a noisy hilarious chorus from the crowd yet thirsting for his blood. Not until five o'clock in the afternoon was Casati released from those bonds and led away to prison, from whence, after a few days, he escaped, and reached with great difficulty the border of Lake Albert. There he was met by a troop of 1000 savages armed with guns and lances, who would certainly have taken his life, had he not been protected by a friendly chief.

The wrath of Cabrega pursued him even there, and the inhabitants received orders to give this enemy of the nation and his companions no food, and not to let them pass.

They were expelled from every village they entered, and beaten. Hungry and thirsty, they marched through muddy places, going down to their knees in the holes made by the feet of the hippopotami; forcing their way through woven masses of vines, and walking through wastes of high reeds, now going out of the way or crouching down to avoid some large amphibious animal. No food had been given them except some beans prepared secretly by a young Dinca woman married to the chief, who pitied them. The situation became more serious every day, and they would have perished if they had not been at last relieved from fatigue, hunger, thirst, and anxious fear, by the steamer sent up the lake to rescue them by Emin. But the joy of meeting was soon obscured by reproaches which Casati felt to be unjust.

He had accomplished his mission with zeal, prudence, dignity, and wisdom, without intrigue and without cowardice, and felt wounded to be treated like a child on his return by the friend who should have been grateful. Almost the first words of Casati to Emin, when aboard the steamer Khedive on Lake Albert, were, 'Stanley has arrived.' Fifteen days before, while still a prisoner in Unioro, Casati had heard the natives speak of the apparition, in the country of Valegga, of Europeans with many armed men dressed like the people of Zanzibar.

Emin, after attacking many of the tribes on the lake, moved on in search of Stanley, who was in need himself of aid. Casati advised Emin after attending to this duty, and thanking Stanley for the heroic effort, to retire by way of the River Obangi-Maqua-Uelle, through Mambettù, a friendly country. But his counsel was not accepted, and a more disastrous route was selected for the return.

THE END.

www.ingramcontent.com/pod-product-compliance
Lightning Source LLC
Chambersburg PA
CBHW020919230426
43666CB00008B/1506